ON SHOW

TEMPORARY DESIGN FOR FAIRS, SPECIAL EVENTS, AND ART EXHIBITIONS

GINGKO PRESS

ON SHOW
TEMPORARY DESIGN FOR FAIRS, SPECIAL EVENTS, AND ART EXHIBITIONS

ISBN 978-1-58423-494-4

First Published in the United States of America by Gingko Press
by arrangement with Sandu Publishing Co., Limited

Gingko Press, Inc.
1321 Fifth Street
Berkeley, CA 94710 USA
Tel: (510) 898 1195
Fax: (510) 898 1196
Email: books@gingkopress.com
www.gingkopress.com

Copyright © 2012 by SANDU PUBLISHING

First published in 2012 by Sandu Publishing

Sponsored by Design 360°
– Concept and Design Magazine

Edited and produced by
Sandu Publishing Co., Ltd.

Book design, concepts & art direction by
Sandu Publishing Co., Ltd.

sandu.publishing@gmail.com
www.sandupublishing.com

Cover illustration by Nendo

Printed and bound in China

PREFACE

EPHEMERAL ARCHITECTURE
New Field of Experimentation

By **Hector Ruiz Velazquez**

Architecture gains a new disciplinary perspective through its association with brands of all sectors in launching their commercial projects. The involvement of the existing skin of the products transcends the mere function of show casing and gets to temporary exhibition spaces and fairs of maximum media attraction.

The rapid pace of growth experienced by large commercial companies over the last decade illustrates the needs of the postmodern consumer who is lost and tangled by the infinite possibilities of choice. This has led marketing departments to develop a complex system of sales techniques. These techniques are designed to encourage purchasing decisions and try to offer the consumer experiences that allow them to identify with the product and transcend the mere function of offering a product.

The variety, sophistication and creativity adopted in these techniques do not only reflect the high degree of maturity of the commercial sector but also the rapid development that this sector has experienced. In a world where culture and consumption are intertwined and break the boundaries that had separated them, architects enter to work in and experience these commercial ephemeral spaces. Through this, sales efforts become great commercial experiences and thereby increase sales.

It's very interesting to see the result of many of these ephemeral containers designed for important fairs; to see how they mix in clever functionality with various aspects such as art, culture, psychology, sociology and many other aspects of urban architecture, allowing consumers to socialize in a familiar way with the brand. This mixture of elements in ephemeral architecture converts it into a tool for successful sales; something already known in history, for example, the way the Romans used to play with the intelligentsia and marketing in their architecture to sell their own Modus Vivendi.

The aim of these ephemeral containers is to replace the passive presentation of a product or service by an active presentation. They help to transform purchasing from a mere economic transaction into a unique, almost mystical, experience - an interesting approach that dissolves the boundaries between brand and customer and between firm and buyer.

We find exhibition spaces that reflect the hybrid, mestizo, flexible and changeable world in which we live. For this reason large companies in their marketing departments use architecture as a commercial tool.

It creates a site of convergence for customers, products, and brands - but it is also the place where the transmission of the brand's values gains strength and potential. This type of construction acquires, because of its temporal characteristics, a unique spatial dimension. It condenses in record time the purpose of showing the great potential of the product and then justifying an intensive business process to the point of sale. A gratifying and productive tandem between architecture and industry emerges in a fair process. The commitment taken by the architect in the exposure of a brand or product multiplies the value of mere display of the offer,

beyond the potential of advertising and other brand communications.

The result of these ephemeral containers is the profusion of materials: hard, soft, thick, technological, smooth, transparent, opaque. Games of perspective and large scale visual languages convert the space into an overwhelming sensory experience focusing on one idea through all forms of communication. These are spaces that are designed for experiences, storytelling, hearing, tasting, and feeling. Despite the undeniable role of visual factors in commercial seduction, other channels of perception have been increasingly incorporated into ephemeral architecture to make it a great communication venue.

Architecture that has traditionally been a distant minority discipline, apart from commercial factors, now starts partnering with the consumer system and becomes a reflection of our time. We create culture through consumption and consume through culture.

CONTENTS

The designers favor uniqueness and desirable ways of experiencing space. Spaces that sharpen brand awareness, and encourage the consumer to become a 'brand messenger'. Company logo, figurative mark, graphic stylistic devices and typography form a consistent unit. The argyle as a design principle consists of a rhombus and a grid structure. The design concept was based on providing room for interpretation to the traditional recognition feature of Burlington. The playful and colorful handling of the graphic pattern element is the identification element and manifestation of the layout principle. The argyle becomes physically palpable and the main feature of the design. The three-dimensionality of the concept results in an intermediary space in which lights and shadows interplay. A colorlayer, which covers the actual construction, the furniture, and the relief wall is like a second skin, providing the opportunity for repeated redefinitions. In the center of the fair stand you find a meeting point, which we call 'meltingpot'. It's a place where people converge, where companies, distributors, and consumers come together. On display: new patterns, new collections, new accessories of upcoming seasons.

BURLINGTON PREMIUM A
KEGGENHOFF I PARTNER

DESIGN / KEGGENHOFF I PARTNER
PHOTOGRAPHY / Constantin Meyer, Köln
LOCATION / Premium, Berlin, Germany

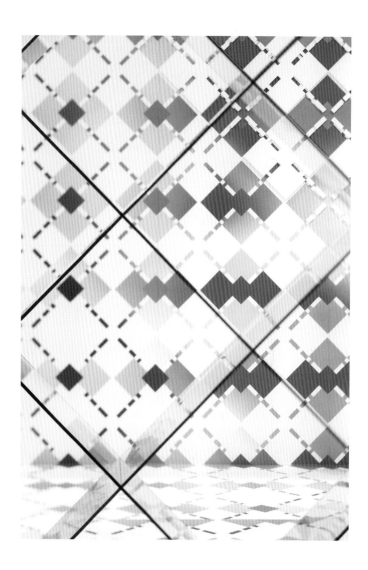

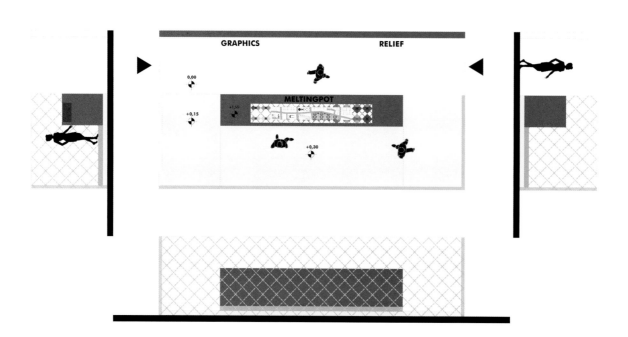

Wall panels with slits which are then slotted into one another -
like the slotted card game "House of Cards" designed by Charles
Eames - form the framework for the modular wall system. All the
surfaces have the same cross-section and the slits are thus also
the same. The very high room elements can be slotted together
without tools and are held together- without any additional
fasteners - by their own weight. They are reminiscent of folding
screens which can be placed anywhere and easily dismantled. These
elements are used to create rooms which offer enough space for
every subject of the collection. FALKE focuses on visual, reduced
clarity as well as relieving formal ballast through a sensitive
seriousness towards the chosen idiom. The goal is to create a
natural analogy, its abstraction and interpretation as aesthetic,
physical and psychological refreshment.

The exterior of the booth is intentionally unspectacular; it is
not until the visitor steps on the glossy black floor of the
interior that he is confronted with the complexity of the room
and the strong colors of the products. Clear view relationships
and axes make orientation simple, create depth and structure the
overlapping (functional) levels.

FALKE ESS

KEGGENHOFF I PARTNER

DESIGN / KEGGENHOFF I PARTNER
PHOTOGRAPHY / Constantin Meyer, Köln
LOCATION / Premium, Berlin, Germany

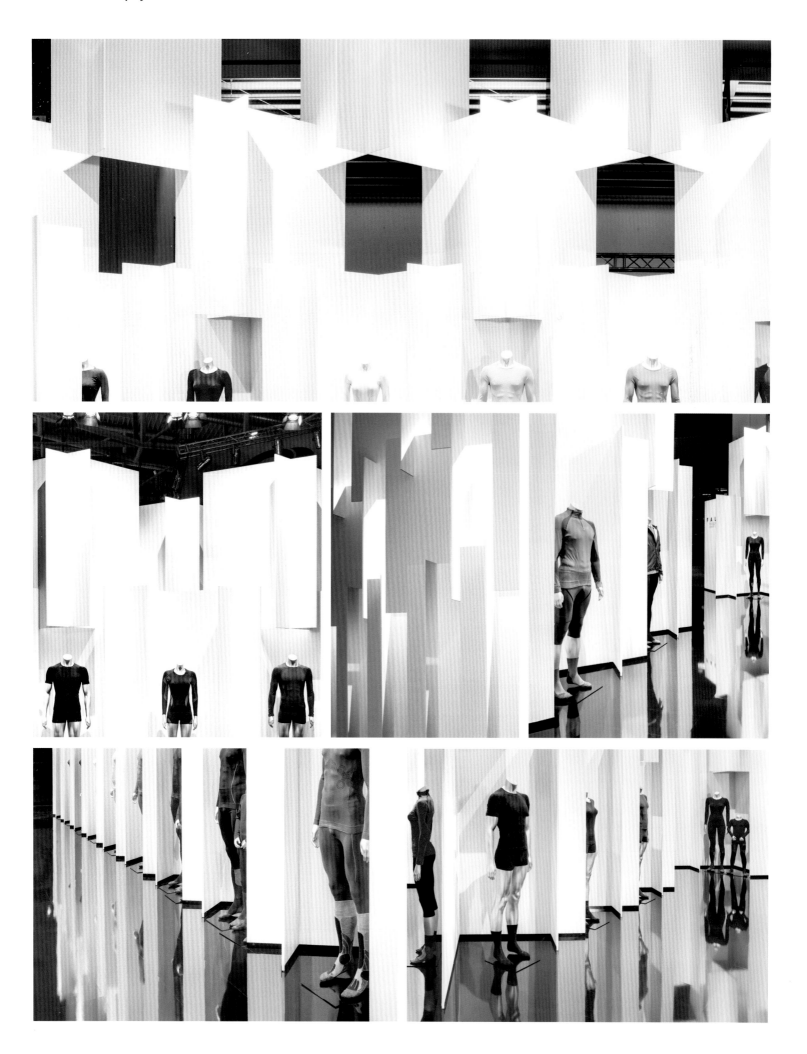

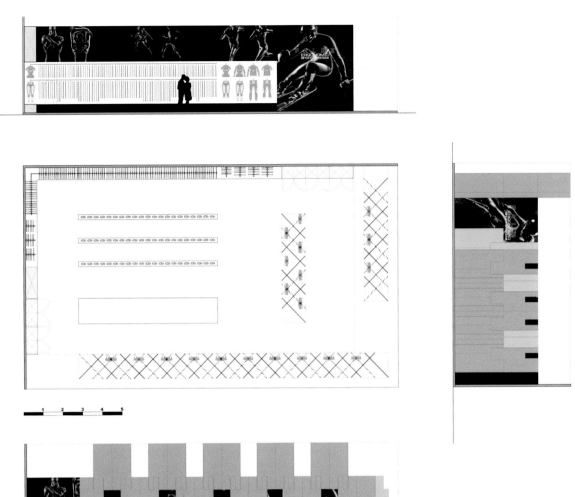

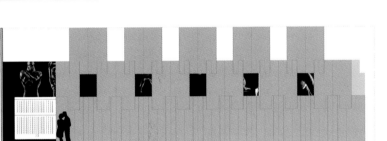

The proper features of the brand: Freedom - at the same time ironic, surprising, creative, timeless, individual, free-thinking, progressive, confident, open, exceptional, complex and at no time uniform. Apart from this there is dedication to quality, attention to detail and inducing impulse.

The color themes associated with black and rural white are used associatively and symbolically. First they are compared mentally, then spatially. The connecting elements of proportion, space and detail, form and material shall be comprehended and apprehended sensually.

The conceptual basis of the segment WHITE aims at consumers with a personal affinity that is deemed to be sporty, nonchalant, casual and rural - a cultural collage. The materiality of the surroundings is characterized by wood, the systematics of the allocation shows certain unrest, the structure is laminated and the presentation is rather fragmented. The atmospheric impression is lively and playful. In summary the tradition plays the focusing role.

The conceptual basis of the segment BLACK aims at consumers with a personal affinity that is deemed to be noble, pure, simple, and urban. The materiality of the surrounding structure is characterized by metal, the systematics of the allocation show a precise order, the structure is visible as a successive movement and the presentation is to be understood as a large scale bracket. The atmospheric impression is quiet and calm, the details are precise, perfected and linear. In summary it is clear that modernity, timelessness and clarity are the most important parameters - an individual, confident style.

BURLINGTON PREMIUM B
KEGGENHOFF I PARTNER

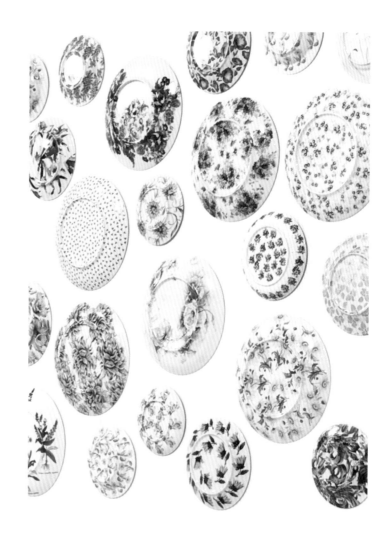

DESIGN / KEGGENHOFF I PARTNER
PHOTOGRAPHY / Constantin Meyer, Köln
LOCATION / Premium, Berlin, Germany

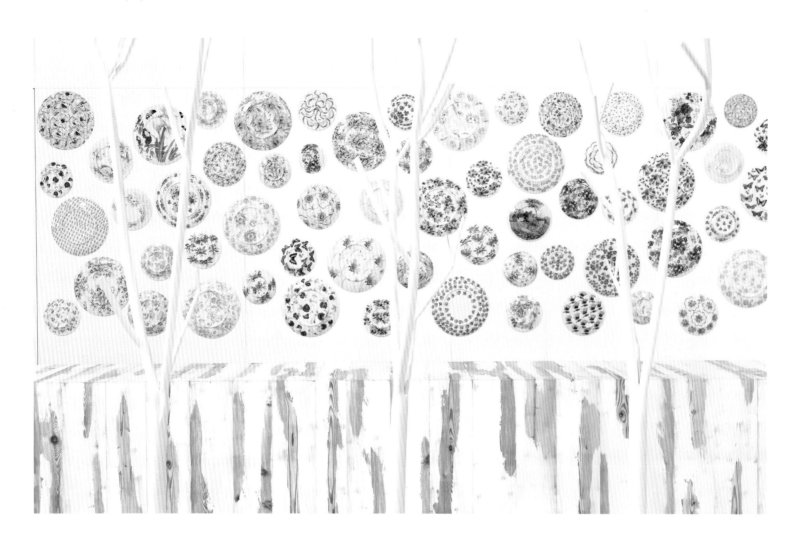

The Smart-ologic Corian Living exhibition gave the designer the opportunity to develop a modular holistic house - a house that can be produced with minimal concave and convex panels and simple tooling. The designer believed that the design of Smart-ologic Corian Living is a metaphor for how technology, housing, furnishing, and space can work together to evoke an increased sense of experience, affect people's psyche and bring us a better living, and also enable the designer to reduce the environmental imprint of our daily decisions and actions.

Smart-ologic Corian Living for Dupont

Karim Rashid Inc.

DESIGN / Karim Rashid
PHOTOGRAPHY / Leo Torri
LOCATION / Milan, Italy

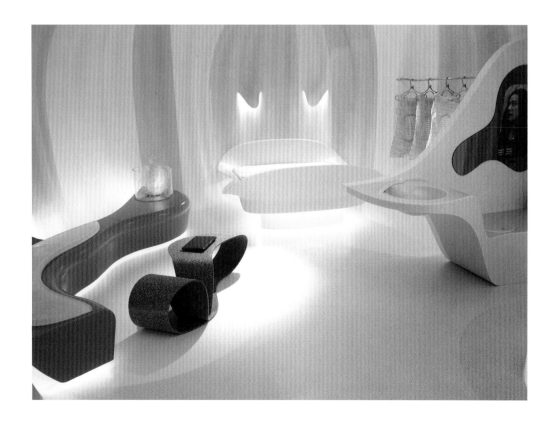

Aesop has created an installation in Hong Kong's I.T HYSAN ONE flagship store that builds on the reputation for architecturally remarkable retail spaces. The installation is also operated as a counter.

Cheungvogl architects, inspired by a black and white image of hundreds of floating lanterns, have imbued the I.T HYSAN ONE exhibition space with a similar delicate luminosity. Eight hundred resin boxes are arranged atop steel rods of varying lengths, creating the sense that each box is ascending at its own pace, as if being drawn upward by an invisible thread. Some boxes hold Aesop formulations while others are designed to reward visitors' curiosity through unexpected sound, scent and touch.

At the end of its two-week tenure the Aesop installation will be deconstructed and re-formed as a permanent counter on the first floor of I.T HYSAN ONE.

Aesop I.T Installation
Cheungvogl Architects Ltd.

DESIGN / Judy Cheung, Christoph Vogl
PHOTOGRAPHY / Cheungvogl Architects
LOCATION / Hong Kong, China

Sony confirmed their leadership position by astonishing the world with their very first 3D home television entertainment system. The best way to tell people about new technology is fairly simple: let them try it out. Real-time demo time!

Mo Ka added a new dimension to the concept of 'tryvertising' by creating a demo-booth that played with the idea of 3D itself: shifting plates, deconstructed design, and trompe l'oeil effects were used to ease visitors into the idea of discovering a whole new world. They were the chosen ones, entering new territory, where the old rules no longer apply. The design itself was slick and glossy, in keeping with the Sony brand and in keeping with the target audience of smart, influential, fun-seeking early adopters.

Inside the booth were 2 fully functional 'theatres' where the visitors experienced the full HD 3D television optimal conditions.

Mo Ka also styled and selected the perfect hosts to guide visitors into the 3D-TV-era.

Sony 3D World
MO KA

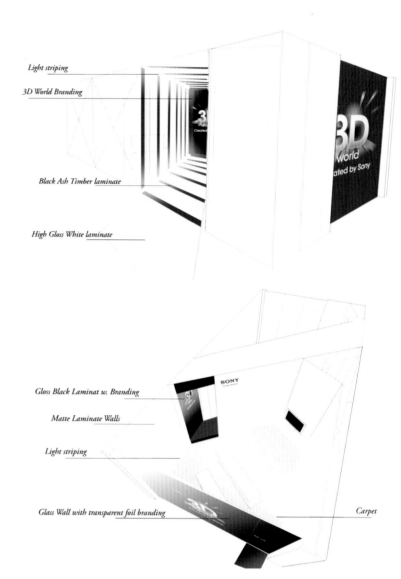

DESIGN / Tim Peters, Catherine Specht, Gunter Durant
PHOTOGRAPHY / MO KA
LOCATION / Brussels, Belgium

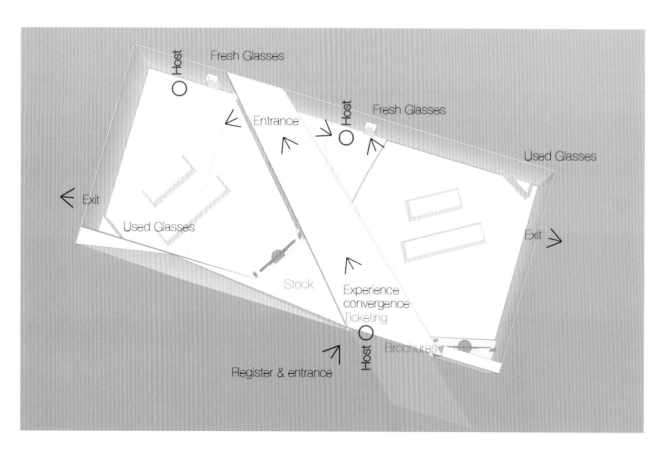

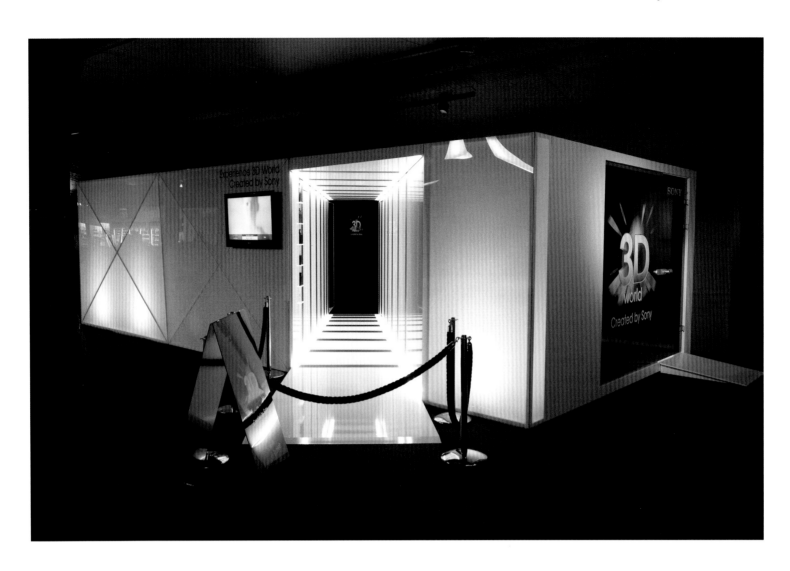

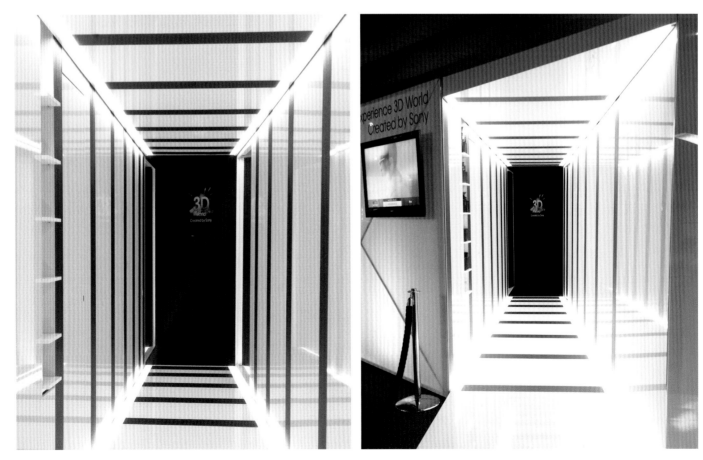

'Lift yourself up from your everyday existence and step literally into the pages of a magazine'. What's real and what isn't? Reading a magazine transports the reader's mind from ordinary, day-to-day life to another place and time, to another world full of wonder. In the 101 house, you literally step into the pages of a magazine, giving you an experience that you will never forget. Create your perfect world with this 'Draw your own environment' concept.

The design concept was 'Folding two-dimensional sheets of paper to create a three-dimensional world'. In the 101 house, shapes, elements and objects are abstracted, arranged (in layers, just like in a peep box, with different heights and volumes), and sometimes taken out of context (such as scale increases on objects such as lights, cups etc.). Odd, yet recognizable. An exciting interplay of shapes, surfaces and textures, like in the composition of a painting. A large, floating roof provides seclusion and the semi-transparent ceiling filters the light, creating a unique atmosphere inside.

Implementation of this sketched world creates a unique environment. The lines are drawn by hand and vary in width. The lines are drawn in a rough style and have an abstract, graphical character. They are sometimes decorated with subtle designs, and sometimes left blank. The theme of the sketches is realistic, humorous and feminine in nature (in accordance with the target audience). The drawings tell a story and/or leave an impression on the viewer. Suggestive lines and sketches are drawn on the walls and floors, but also on furniture and other objects. What's real and what isn't?

101 woonideeën
INGRID HEIJNE INTERIOR DESIGN

DESIGN / Ingrid Heijne
PHOTOGRAPHY / Hugo Thomassen
LOCATION / Amsterdam, the Netherlands

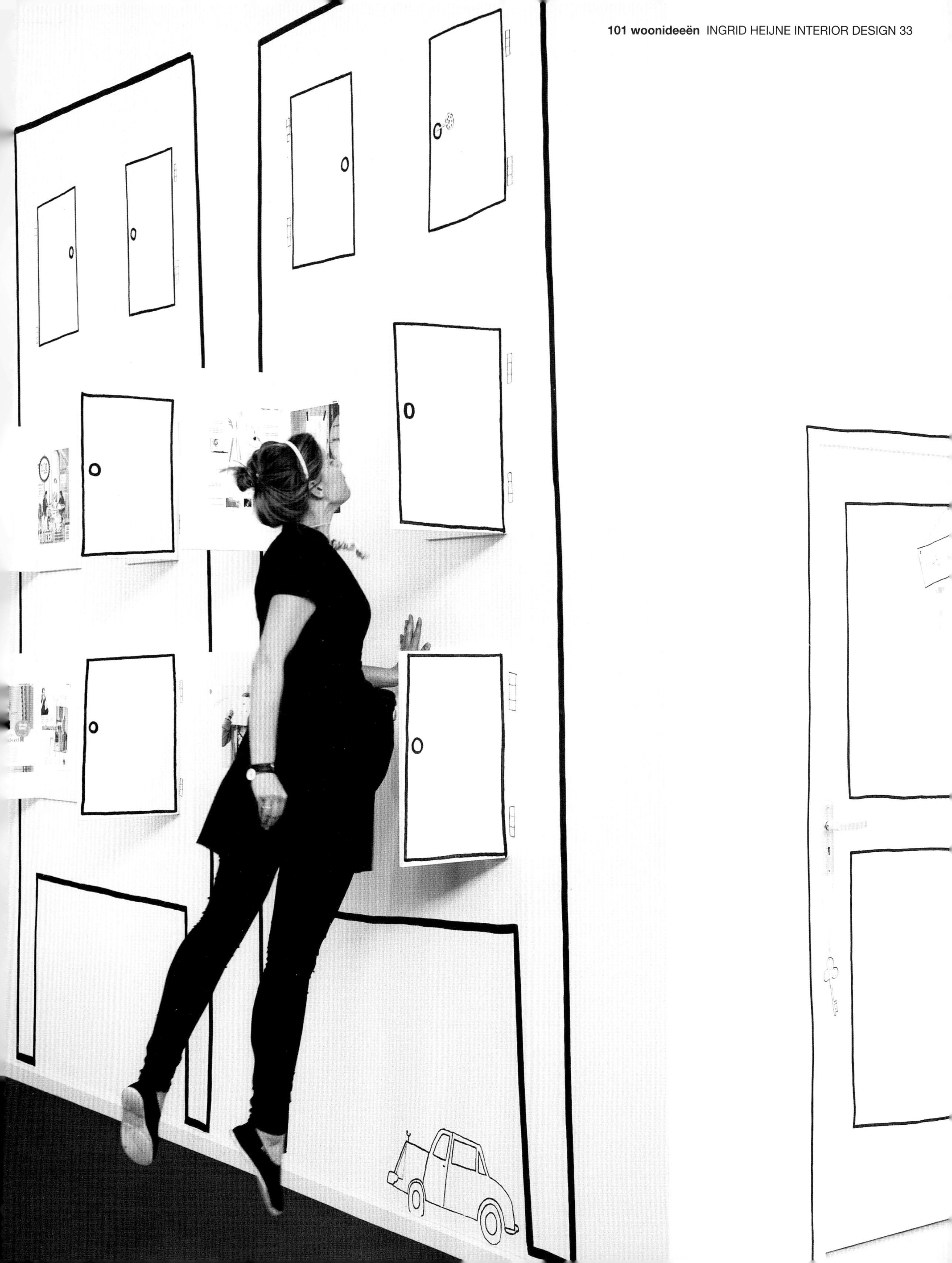

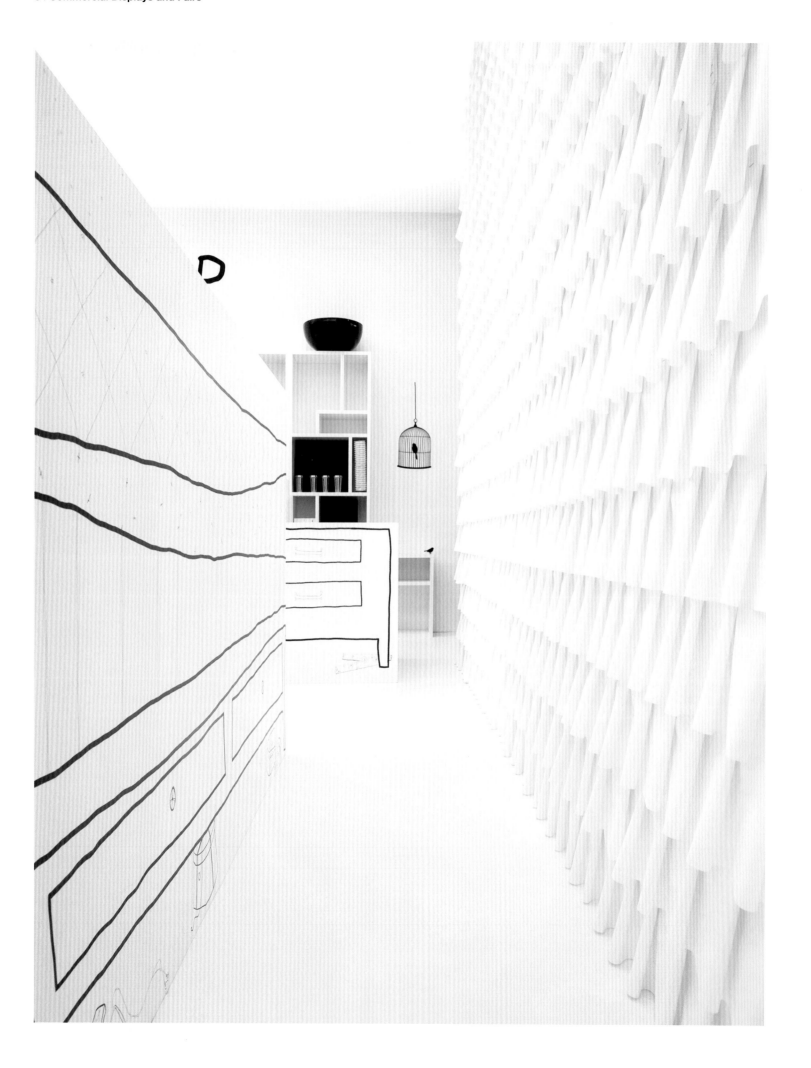

Burkhardt Leitner develops, produces and distributes modular architecture systems for temporary constructions employed in trade fair, exhibition and presentation design. Burkhardt Leitner architecture systems combine a high degree of functionality with exceptional flexibility, making them easily adaptable to customer requirements. Burkhardt Leitner used the EuroShop 2011 to introduce two new architecture systems to its international sales partners and potential customers. The challenge was to present the company and its products in an appealing and striking manner.

Epitomising the 'fantastic – systematic' claim, the Burkhardt Leitner stand transforms the minimalist functionality of its spatial systems and its core brand values of precision, lightness, sustainability, flexibility and mobility into a playful and atmospheric stage set.

The exhibition stand is an impressive illustration of how Burkhardt Leitner systems provide the perfect spatial platform for exceptionally creative brand staging.

The stand demonstrates how Burkhardt Leitner modular systems can be transformed into a creative playground and unfurl their full atmospheric potential. Wholly in line with the company's brand-defining practical minimalism, simple, reduced construction elements contrast boldly with amusing ornamental details to set striking accents. With dynamic, three-dimensional walls, tactile surfaces, ingenious graphics and surprising changes of vantage point, the Burkhardt Leitner stand invites visitors to explore its multifaceted constructive and decorative nuances.

Burkhardt Leitner Construktiv – EuroShop 2011

Ippolito Fleitz Group – Identity Architects

DESIGN / Ippolito Fleitz Group
PHOTOGRAPHY / Zooey Braun
LOCATION / Düsseldorf, Germany

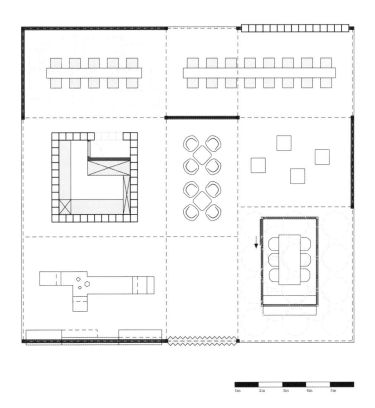

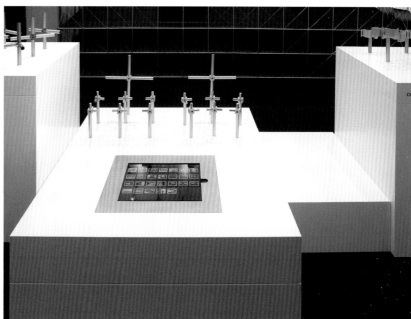

As the leading global bathroom brand, industry front runner Roca proves once again how strong its brand and products are at this year's preeminent trade fair, the ISH in Frankfurt. Designed by dan pearlman, the 895 square meters stand conveys a sense of dynamism and motion. Based on the theme Moving Forward, the design makes use of curving corridors and expressively highlighted slanting surfaces in getting its message across.

Mediacore – Heart of the Brand Presentation: In the middle of the stand a 360° media projection allows visitors to enter into the Roca world. Viewers are immersed in the everyday expression of the brand's congenial messages and experience the "bathroom living space" in a highly realistic manner. The Roca world is just as multi-faceted as the range of Roca products. On twenty-six square meters the rectangular cube reflects all Roca themes and guides one through an extensive product presentation.

Rich Black Dominates: Alongside the corporate color a glowing white makes for dynamic light-dark contrasts. A focused selection of materials also plays off of the contrasts between dark smoked oak and light-toned concrete. In the Roca Lounge on the upper level of the two-storey stand, maple wood creates a warm and inviting ambience.

Roca Trade Fair Stand
dan pearlman Markenarchitektur GmbH

DESIGN / dan pearlman Markenarchitektur GmbH
PHOTOGRAPHY / diephotodesigner.de
LOCATION / Frankfurt am Main, Germany

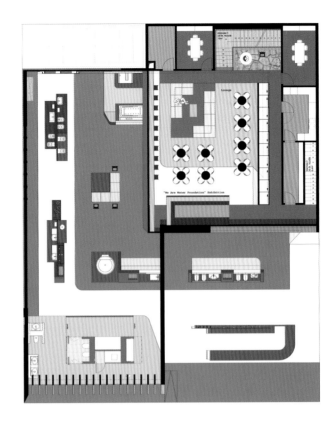

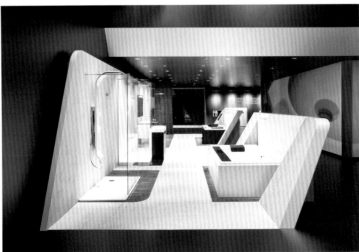

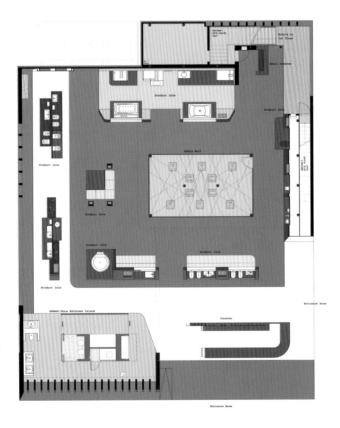

Opportunity: To help with the brand's reposition in the vanguard field, generating a measurable return in terms of wide knowledge and sales.

Solution: Culdesac™ has designed an environment where you can play endlessly with lights and mirrors, creating a surface of optical illusion. A conventional room becomes a broad space around us with its vastness and takes us to a sea of tranquility. The atmosphere takes you back to antiquity, the era in which philosophers promoted the search for tranquility necessary for a happy and enjoyable life in which fear had no place to target. A life made for enjoying every second with all its intensity. In this space of serenity the protagonist is a visitor and all the elements are arranged to provide a moment of reflection. Roca presents an atmosphere of innovation, design, sound quality and comfort.

Results: Roca defined its strategic vision for the future, and began a process of internal transformation in order to achieve: Vision 2020 (V2020) bases its philosophy on a compendium of measures that serve to visualize, define and create groundbreaking spaces.

ARAB BATHS

Culdesac

DESIGN / Culdesac
PHOTOGRAPHY / Culdesac
LOCATION / Barcelona, Spain

Die Stuttgart Region is one of the most important economic centres in Europe. The trade fair concept translates the specific duality of stability and growth into one metaphoric icon – the modern interpretation of a tree dynamically striving upward and yet steadfastly rooted in the earth. As a symbol for stability and "grounding", the floors and the furnishings of the stand were made of solid materials in matching earth tones. The expansive "treetop" made of oversized silver cubes represents growth and dynamics. Imprinted motifs reflect the many facets of the region.

Wirtschaftsförderung Region Stuttgart ExpoReal

Ippolito Fleitz Group
– Identity Architects

DESIGN / Ippolito Fleitz Group
PHOTOGRAPHY / Zooey Braun
LOCATION / Germany

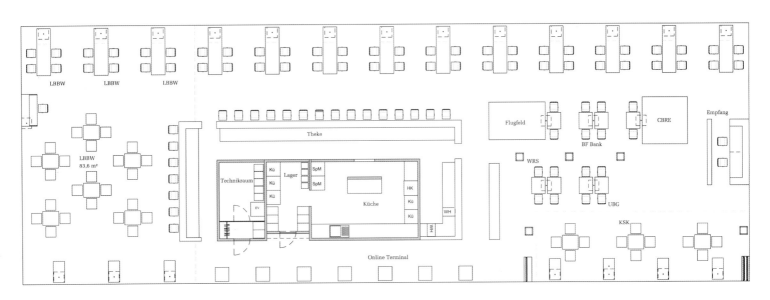

A vineyard inside a museum. For the House of History Baden-Wurttemberg ATELIER BRÜCKNER, realized a special exhibition which shows the wine scenery of Baden-Wurttemberg clearly and informatively. The expressive room narrative was derived from the structure of a vineyard. 495 ground tests presented in glass cylinders and the accompanying end product, a full bottle of wine, are rhythmically arranged like vines to a spatially dynamic structure featuring cohesive scenery that represents the individuality of the region, local winegrowers, and cultivation methods.

The individuality is tangible at first sight with the help of the different grounds and the bottle creation. Besides, in well-chosen cylinders winegrowers report in video installations about their wine-growing methods and strategies remains competitive in the global wine market.

The exhibit cubes which are sprinkled like small vineyard houses into the great structure are devoted to cultural-historical subjects revolving around fermented grape juice. Here it is about species of vines, cooperatives, wine drinkers and wine experts, wine measuring and about the effects of environmental factors on the wine cultivation. It becomes clear that in Baden-Wurttemberg not mass, but variety and individuality counts. This individuality stands in an optically produced contrast to an anonymous wine shelf which forms the Entrée to the exhibit. It represents the huge number of European and non-European wines which likewise fill our wine glass.

Serve Pure Wine
– Wineworld in Change
ATELIER BRÜCKNER

DESIGN / ATELIER BRÜCKNER
PHOTOGRAPHY / Bernd Eidenmüller
LOCATION / Württemberg, Stuttgart, Germany

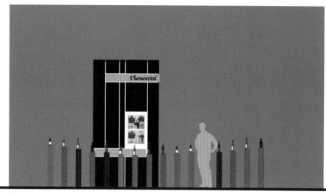

Themenvitrine 1

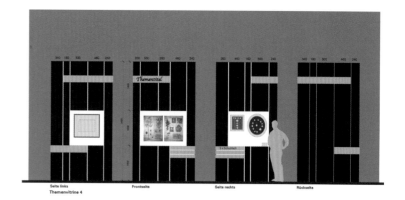

Seite links
Themenvitrine 4   Frontseite   Seite rechts   Rückseite

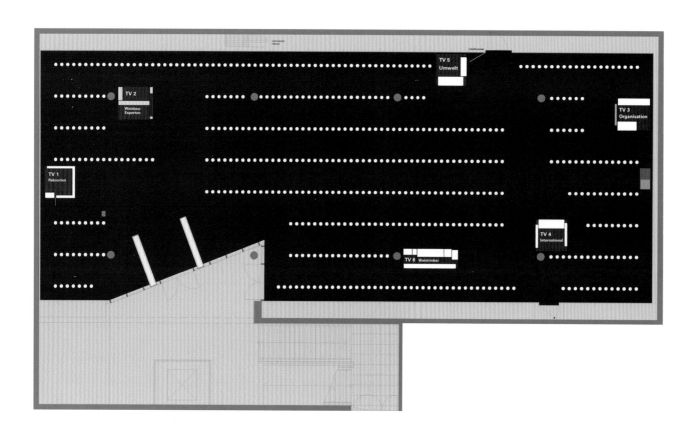

WELTWEIT

WEINTRINKER

A brand staging was developed that hinged on stylish orchestration of the themes of art, fashion and clubbing to appeal to the trend setters from post-Modern milieus, the main MINI target group.

The cube structure references the dimensions of the vehicle premiering and with its textile material feel on the inside and outside (fabric-covered facades and felt-covered floor and seating systems) communicates the car's image while also highlighting fashion.

The entrance area is characterized by a low slit that serves as a magnet attracting visitors.

On the inside, the staged space points up the perspectives – featuring as the central element the "MINI Clubman Catwalk" as a quotation from the fashion world. Atmospheric use of the space is achieved via the two flanking interactive audio-visual media walls on the two sides, offering artistic themes from the world of Pop, mixed with bizarre figures and graphic devices. The installation is controlled in real time by a VJ with live feeds from material shot in the blue box. Seating areas on both sides invite visitors to chill out and create a setting for a shared experience of the MINI brand community.

The entire inside area consists of a dovetailed space that oscillates between fashion, art and clubbing, structured in the MINI Lifestyle Shop, with the fashion items suspended from illuminated hangers in the air to reference contemporary shopping worlds, the MINI International Bar as a monochrome, dripping, red space, and the complementary interactive Blue Box with the GoKart Simulator.

Catwalk
Franken Architekten GmbH

DESIGN / Franken Architekten GmbH/ Meiré & Meiré
PHOTOGRAPHY / Franken Architekten GmbH
LOCATION / Frankfurt am Main, Germany

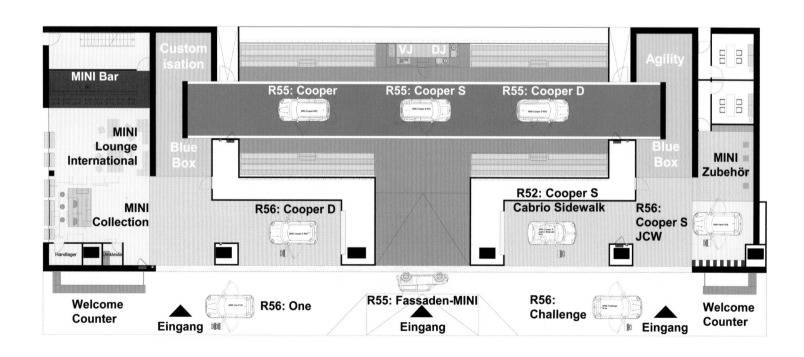

MINI celebrated its 50th birthday in 2009. Its presence at the 2009 IAA international motor show was the MINI birthday party. And a good birthday party means balloons, confetti, cake and guests offering their congratulations. And these ingredients were spread around over-sized letters arranged on two lines, which divided the stand diagonally and which read: WHAT A BIRTHDAY. IT'S MINI.

The lower half of the lettering stood in a single storey on the floor of the hall, while the upper half was suspended from the ceiling and came across as an upper storey, which on one side became a roof suspended freely over a studio area. From the studio a report about the party was broadcast to the world, while in turn the world became part of the party via a video wall. A special guest, the 1959 MINI Minor drove along a red carpet beneath the lettering to the party. In addition video columns were distributed around the stand representing guests offering their congratulations. To mark the event the birthday editions MINI 50 Camden and MINI 50 Mayfair were presented on a double platform. A multi-step sitting area extended from the studio to a lounge, culminating in the MINI International Bar in the rear building wing. This also featured a two-storey lifestyle shop boasting a specially-made Swarovski chandelier.

What A Birthday

Franken Architekten GmbH

DESIGN / Meiré und Meiré/ Franken Architekten GmbH/ Expolab
PHOTOGRAPHY / Franken Architekten GmbH
LOCATION / Frankfurt am Main, Germany

BIG, Kollision and Schmidhuber+Partner teamed up to bring a vision of future urban mobility to life for AUDI at Design Miami/2011, from November 30th to December 4th.

The 190m^2 LED surface illustrates BIG's concept of the future city where infrastructure and public space is shared between pedestrians and driverless cars. The installation demonstrates how the city surface continuously gathers information about people's movements, allowing for real-time interaction between vehicles and the environment.

Kollision developed a real-time graphics engine and tracking software that gets live input from 11 Xbox Kinect cameras mounted above the visitor's heads. The movement of the visitors is processed into patterns of movement displayed on the LED surface. The tracking software is a flexible setup of multiple aligned camera spaces, which are processed and translated by the graphical engine running the visual content on the LED surface. The engine can output a wide range of visual expressions – from a precise vector-like look to a more fluid and playful content. Furthermore the arrow, which illustrates the future movement of the car, is calculated in real-time based on tracking information of people's movements.

The installation sets the stage for Audi's A2 concept car, which had its U.S debut at the design fair and which is dedicated to the future of urban mobility and capable of communicating with its environment.

Urban Future
BIG, Kollision, Schmidhuber+Partner

DESIGN / Big and Kollision
PHOTOGRAPHY / Big and Kollision
LOCATION / Miami, USA

BMW World is the adventure and delivery center for the BMW brand. The company opted for a design by COOP HIMMELB(L)AU which particularly embodied the dynamism and innovation of the brand.

For dan pearlman and in cooperation with BMW, the objective was to fill this building with life and integrate the brand's strengths - innovation, emotion, precision, dynamism and aesthetics. Guests experience BMW as part of a greater exhibition of all vehicles. They sense the passion of motorbike riding and see technical and design-related topics communicated with feeling.

The horizon is our destination
Throughout all stages of the car exhibition - developed by dan pearlman- the guest experiences an emotional and theatrical presentation. The car is the star - the vehicles are displayed on stages assigned to thematic areas. Each theme is made intuitively accessible to the guests.

Driving Pleasure
Exhibits are used to make technology and design-related themes interactively and intuitively accessible. Here, the pioneering spirit of BMW is in the air and perfection can be felt in every detail.

If sheer driving pleasure is essential to the BMW, for the BMW Motorcycle it epitomizes a whole philosophy of life. dan pearlman unfolded an extensive study as part of the product and brand dramatization. The solutions developed form a prestigious shop window for the brand: from the product experience to the communication of brand values and the embedding of motorcycles in emotional worlds.

BMW Welt
dan pearlman Markenarchitektur GmbH

DESIGN / dan pearlman
PHOTOGRAPHY / dan pearlman
LOCATION / Munich, Germany

The advertisement agency wire asked the designers to develop a media packed, spatial design for the Mercedes-Benz Service unit. Heller Designstudio extended the existing pixelated campaign to a 3-dimensional experience. The exhibition cubes are filled with the latest technologies and services the unit has to offer. The users are able to explore the content in an interactive way.

Mercedes-Benz Service IAA
Heller Designstudio

DESIGN / Heller Designstudio
PHOTOGRAPHY / Pia Schweisser
LOCATION / Frankfurt am Main, Germany

dan pearlman bred a future generation of interior design in the CREATE Berlin showroom and Epiphytes are not fixed pieces of furniture, in fact they are unique hybrid creatures of polygonal shape and organic evolution.

They connect with interior spaces as growing vegetation, ornamental adornments, or functional solutions. The living ground areas of adaptable exotics are almost boundless: they are capable of permeating virtual and real spaces by forming a multi-dimensional living and adventure system as well as in the carbon world. They enter into a fruitful symbiosis with the denizens of both realities; interaction defines the comfort of living. The scaling of these extraordinary organisms defines their functionality, the standards of humans and avatars determine the parameters of their performance, and their production takes place on demand. Epiphytes enable a mixed reality to be intuitively experienced.

The forward looking assimilation of both habitats defines not only creation and experience, but also development, manufacturing (digital crafts) and materiality of the binary botanical organisms. The correlation between 3d-CAD design, 5-axis simultaneous CNC technique and state-of-the-art Corian® material is steering an innovative development process.

Epiphytes - Polymorphic Breeding Furniture

dan pearlman Markenarchitektur GmbH

DESIGN / Volker Katschinski
PHOTOGRAPHY / diephotodesigner.de
LOCATION / Berlin, Germany

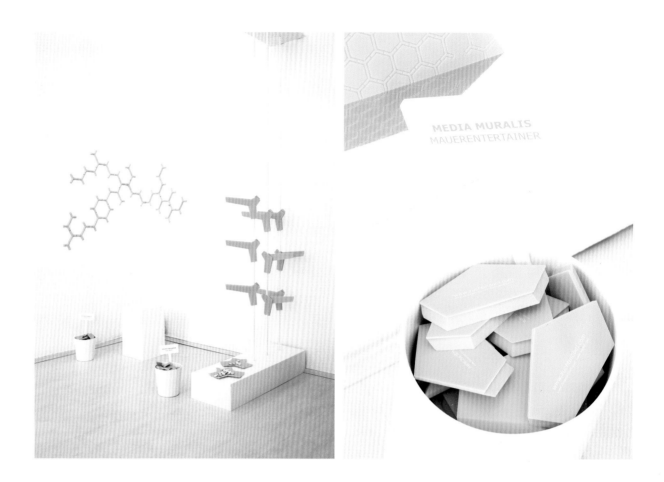

MEDIA MURALIS
MAUERENTERTAINER

Brunner is a prestigious manufacturer of utility furniture with a main focus on furniture for events, conventions and nursing homes. This family-run company has made a name for itself in custom-made furniture that is precisely tailored towards customer requirements. In the context of a strategic brand repositioning, the furniture manufacturer wishes to position itself more strongly as an architectural brand. The Brunner exhibition stand at the Orgatec 2010 was expressly designed to underscore this new positioning.

The exhibition stand features the latest innovations in chairs and conference tables across an area of 390m². The challenge was to portray the brand world as a holistic entity while staging the individual product groups in close, coherent groupings across the elongated, rectangular stand. Translucent gauze ceiling handings were used to create separate layered, flowing sacs. This channeling of attention enables visitors to focus more clearly on the individual products. At the same time, the entire stand always remains visible and comprehensible. The gauzes were hung in strict geometric alignment to recall urban cityscapes.

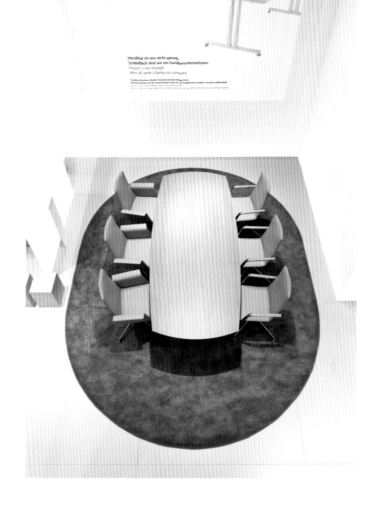

Brunner Fair Stand Orgatec 2010
Ippolito Fleitz Group
– Identity Architects

DESIGN / Ippolito Fleitz Group
PHOTOGRAPHY / bildhübsche fotografie, Andreas Körner
LOCATION / Cologne, Germany

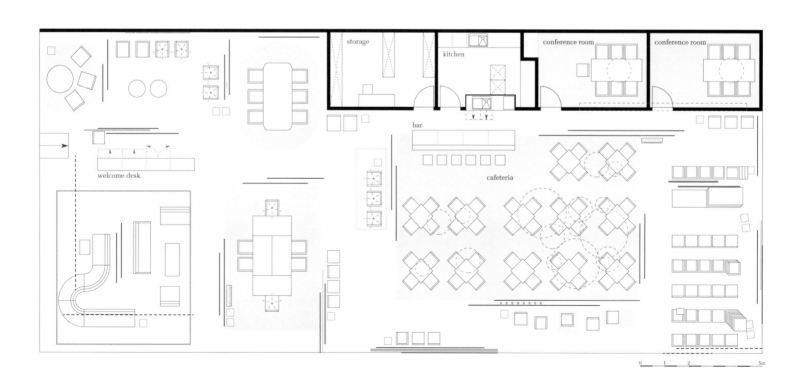

brunner ::

brunner ::

**Mit beiden Beinen auf dem Boden.
Aber den Kopf überall.**
With both feet planted firmly on the ground.
But with our head all over the place.

Wir produzieren ausschließlich in Deutschland aber denken konsequent ohne Grenzen.
So sichern wir höchste Qualität und bleiben immer mutig für neue Ideen, zuverlässig und fair.
We produce exclusively in Germany, but our thinking is resolutely without borders. This is how we ensure
for highest quality and remain always courageous for new ideas, reliable and fair.

brunner ::

**Herzblut ist uns nicht genug.
Schließlich sind wir ein Familienunternehmen.**
Passion is not enough.
After all, we're a family-run company.

Projekte brauchen scharfen Verstand und das richtige Feuer.
Deshalb arbeiten wir für unsere Kunden nicht nur mit Engagement, sondern mit purer Leidenschaft.

www.brunner-group.com

In the 2011 Bangkok Architects' Fair, Diamond Building Products Public Company set up a large scale installation emphasizing their line. Their products are ceramic, laminates, construction hardware, and construction services throughout Thailand. Apostrophys' role in this project was as artistic mastermind for the entire installation. The concept was "Diamond Art - Diamond Lounge 2011." Imagine walking into an aesthetic place, where you leisurely sit and sip some beverages surrounded by art pieces in a gallery made from durable construction hardware pieces. Furthermore, these pieces inspire the visitors to create their own masterpieces in their homes.

This year, the primary use for the Diamond Lounge space is to showcase a demonstration of uses for the Purlin roofing hardware - the highlight of their product launches this year. The designers transformed the Purlin product's functionality into each element of the booth's construction by using the "joint" - a bent angle of Purlin. The main structure is impressive with its large wall and huge lamp ceiling and appears as if the designers actually sketched it out of clean white matte Purlin. The structure casts shadows which create a rhythmic interplay of space and line within the structure. The pavilion is made colorful through the use of strategic lighting by layered hanging LED PAR flourescent light boxes. A programmed pattern of lighting was created which adds another dimension of colorful reflection to the Diamond Lounge.

Diamond Lounge

Apostrophys the Synthesis
Server Co., Ltd.

DESIGN / Apostrophys
PHOTOGRAPHY / Apostrophys
LOCATION / Bangkok, Thailand

The space is located in the Bangkok Design festival 2010 and functions as a game space and a moving landmark for the festival. The space has 22 tubes standing next to each other creating an SCG tree space. On top, it displays connection of branches creating SCG logos.

During the day, the exhibition creates shade during the night, the whole area is lit with colorful lighting which casts interesting shadows. The game classifies each player as Apo-, Co-, Trans-, or Geo-, through a series of questions. Each question corresponds to a tube and as the questions are answered, each tube leads to the next, until the player ends up in a square room in which they are informed which kind of player they are. The space exhibits the pneumatic structural system of a custom-made three branch structure. Each tube is made of fabric with a high pressure side channel blower at the bottom; the process of air passing through is soundless and allows each plastic structure to stand upright like a tree.

A zipper under each blower prevents air from coming out of the tube and changes its form. Each has one LED par inside to create the lighting patterns.

The structure allows the game to be reused after the festival is finished, just like using a questionnaire in many different areas – public spaces, special events, pedestrian bridges etc. They are easy to both install and uninstall without taking up too much storage space.

SCG Booth
Apostrophys the Synthesis Server Co.,Ltd.

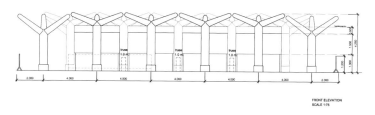

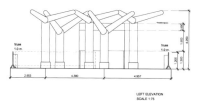

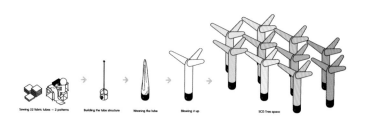

DESIGN / Apostrophys
PHOTOGRAPHY / Apostrophys
LOCATION / Bangkok, Thailand

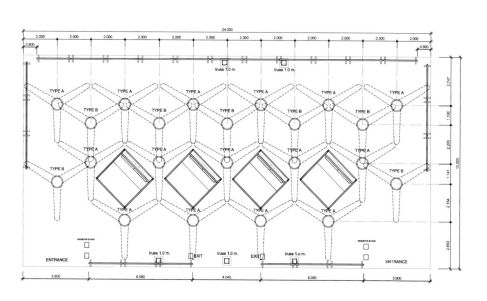

LAY OUT PLAN
SCALE 1:75

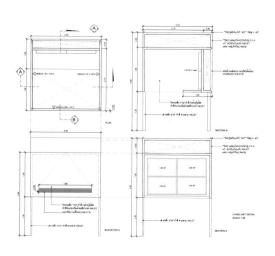

Human beings, especially children, have long felt the need to burrow under a cover or blanket in order to create their own personal space. This playing character is called 'Pee Pa Home' in Thai which means Ghost Blanket which is a fun kind of inspiration brought into the space. By covering ourselves with a blanket, it creates a closed private area with a form that changes when we move. From this, the closed area can be transformed into a space for the public to meet. The basic function of the Art4d Pavilion is to sell Art4d magazines.

The fabric worked as a medium of this fun moving space. It forced the audience to squeeze into the space, sit down, relax and create new communities underneath this single surface. The audience can choose to create their own circle of dialogue.

The different levels of fabric create different volumes for different functions such as spaces for reading, trading, resting and drinking.

The details of the whole structure were considered based on the very limited production and setting up time. For example, the huge zippered panels were used as doors and windows to create an entryway and increase airflow within the space. The zippers were sewed onto the fabric and the bag joints were used to connect the fabric to the floor. All the details are very easy to find and very adaptive.

Art4d Pavilion

Apostrophys the Synthesis
Server Co.,Ltd.

DESIGN / Apostrophys
PHOTOGRAPHY / Apostrophys
LOCATION / Thailand

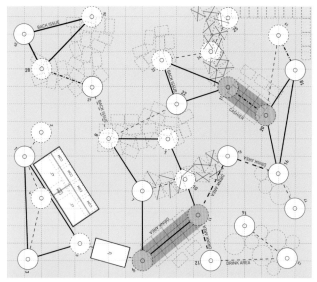

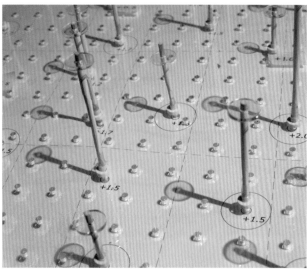

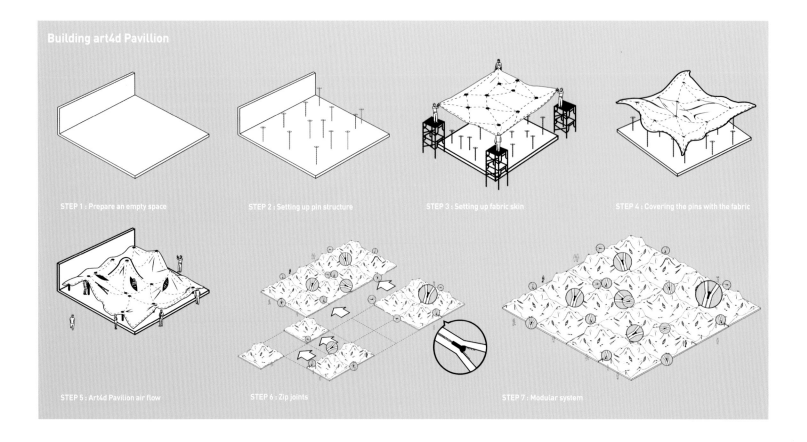

Building art4d Pavillion

STEP 1 : Prepare an empty space

STEP 2 : Setting up pin structure

STEP 3 : Setting up fabric skin

STEP 4 : Covering the pins with the fabric

STEP 5 : Art4d Pavilion air flow

STEP 6 : Zip joints

STEP 7 : Modular system

Geografía Habitable – Outdoor Space - Feria Habitad Valencia

Emerging into this space of light and shade is like entering into a physical allegory of the Spanish geography. This dynamic structure is a total interior surrounding that connects with the exterior thanks to the dynamic forms that evoke the nature of a Made Spain rich in contrasts. This space was designed to wake up the senses of visitors through the vision in different forms, the smell of the real grass in the floor that creates the olfactory sensation of being outdoors, the tactile experience of the living plants growing on the curved walls following the trail, and the sound of a flowing cascade in the heart of the space. The entire installation was built in ten days, all done in a metallic curve structure covered with Acrylic fabric.

This space offers a symbolic vision associated with the soil, the land, the original and authentic. Ramps and elevations are utilized in a balance of unlimited curves.

The space displays elaborately constructed outdoor products which were carefully selected to transport us to a feeling of pleasure and enjoyment of our landscapes and climate. These elaborate products created with innovation, sensitivity, and a competitive vision are the result of our constant search for new ideas and creative design solutions.

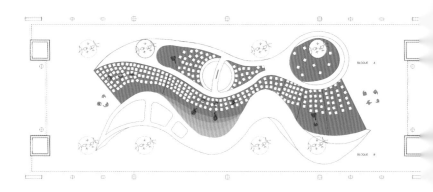

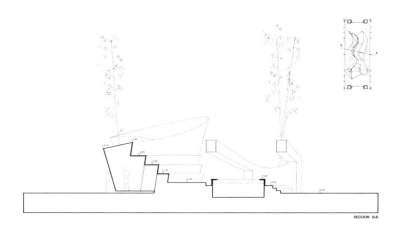

Feria Habitat Valecia
– Geografia Habitable a Collaborator Atefeh Bashir

Ruiz Velazquez Architecture and Design

DESIGN / Hector Ruiz Velazquez
PHOTOGRAPHY / Pedro Martinez
LOCATION / Spain

Living Nature and ECO-DESIGN BUILDING by Hector Ruiz-Velazquez Architecture has an interior space visible through four shop windows (like a small shopping center representing the four types of interior living in Spain). All of the building blocks of the space were created out of cardboard boxes in only 10 days.

The design of a landmark building for an international furniture fair is usually associated with expensive building choices and bizarre shapes, but this building takes design to its original dictation: aesthetics, functionality and low cost. It was designed to be seen and perceived from above, from the outside and from the inside.

Living Nature is a building made with 2000 cardboard boxes and fabric umbrellas for the Habit Valencia International Fair that can be easily assembled and disassembled using only cardboard and screws.

The building holds a central plaza with a pool and a waterfall where the visitors can go away from the mass of people and noise of the fair and enjoy the sunshine and tranquility of the Valencia climate.

The sustainability of Living Nature is not just limited to the material. The ease of assembly, dismantling, and reuse are a great asset of the design. This prevents unnecessary transport and waste materials.

Feria Habitat Valencia-Living Nature
Ruiz Velazquez Architecture and Design

DESIGN / Hector Ruiz Velazquez
PHOTOGRAPHY / Pedro Martinez
LOCATION / Valencia, Spain

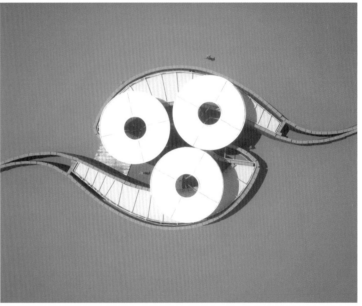

The exhibition creates a zigzag space, created by
1.2 meters × 1.2 meters plywood panels interlocking with each
other. Each presentation is displayed on each panel so visitors
can stop and have a look or just pass through. 7 colors divide the
exhibition into 7 zones according to the fields of design.

Each panel is 1.2 meters × 1.2 meters cut from the standard
1.2 meters × 2.4 meters size of a plywood sheet, to prevent waste
from cutting. Each panel interlocks with each other to create a
stronger structure and be able to stand on its own. The experiment
of its space and structure started from reusing expired invitation
cards to test them and see if they stand on their own by cutting
2 holes on one side to interlock with each other. The card
structure was able to stand on its own and be expanded through
plywood additions. Fluorescent lighting was used for each panel
and colored the space through the use of printed stickers on the
exterior of each lightbulb.

Degree Shows Exhibition

Apostrophys the Synthesis
Server Co., Ltd.

DESIGN / Apostrophys
PHOTOGRAPHY / Apostrophys
LOCATION / Bangkok, Thailand

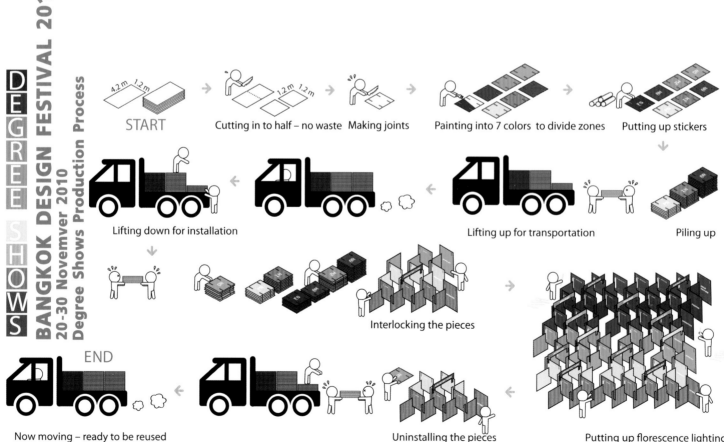

DEGREE SHOWS
BANGKOK DESIGN FESTIVAL 2010
20-30 Novemver 2010
Degree Shows Production Process

4.2 m · 1.2 m
START

Cutting in to half – no waste

Making joints

Painting into 7 colors to divide zones

Putting up stickers

Lifting down for installation

Lifting up for transportation

Piling up

Interlocking the pieces

Putting up florescence lighting

END

Now moving – ready to be reused

Uninstalling the pieces

A good installation project should always consider the audience as an integral part of the scene, making it both spectator and actor; the public should be encouraged to cross the threshold that usually divides the work of art from its audience. Following these criteria, the exhibition at the Triennale di Milano – Teatro dell'Arte, is a total immersion in the world of art photography that Lavazza has developed over the past 20 years of calendars. The screen grabs the scene encompassing part of the audience and projecting on its three-dimensional surface a unique story of travel and seduction that makes use of the project mapping technique. A ladder suspended in the void gives viewers the opportunity to cross the stream of projected images, to pass through the curtain and find themselves in the proscenium area, sucked into a vortex of architecture that reveals every page of this unknown story. A final section will represent the past with the 19 previous calendars, the present with the 2012 calendar with inscription by the respective photographers, and the future with the photographs from the photo scouting talents.

Lavazza con te partirò
Studio Fabio Novembre

DESIGN / Dino Cicchetti, Carlo Formisano, Giorgio Terraneo, Giulio Vescovi
PHOTOGRAPHY / Pasquale Formisano
LOCATION / Milan, Italy

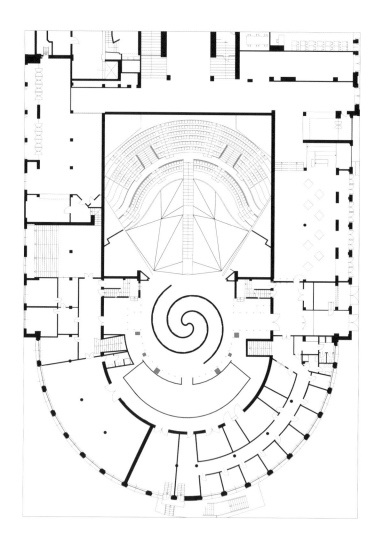

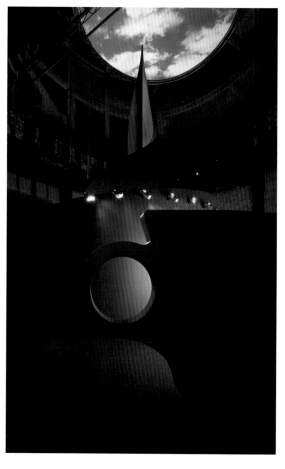

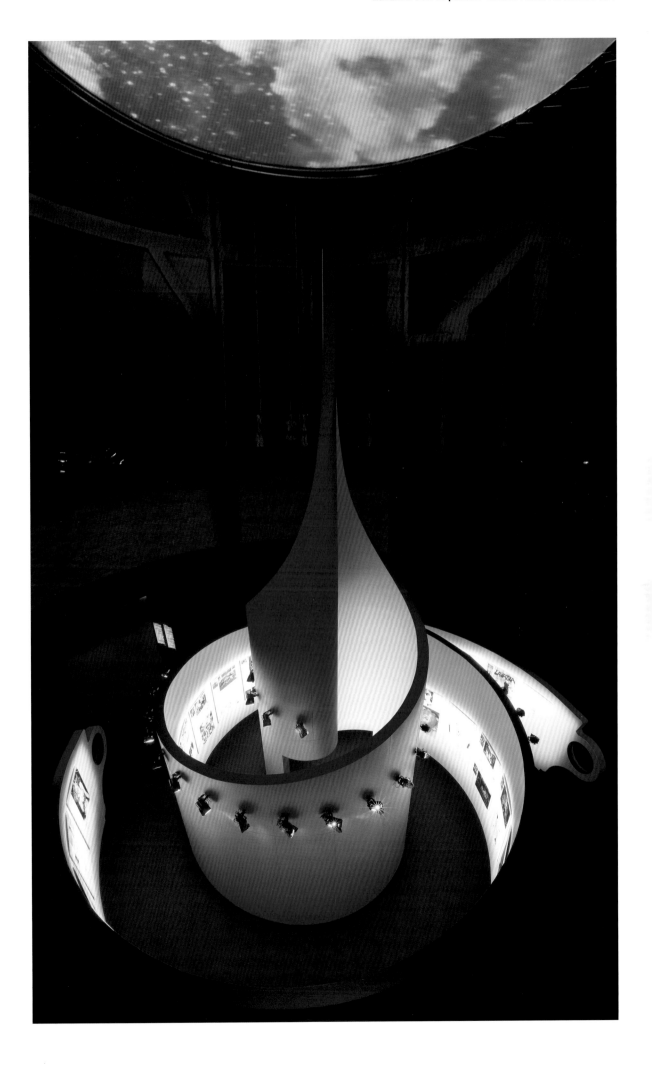

Architecture, furniture and storage all in one. Studio Makkink & Bey took standard sheets of plywood and with CNC cutting, created a miniature house to stand within larger interiors of offices, studios and lofts. With walls of stool, bench and table parts that easily come out and assemble, the functionality and character of the house can be changed as more or less furniture is used.

A poetic vision for efficient production and material use, House of Furniture parts transport flat and can be made to suit different functions, produced locally and customized. Why don't you tell us what your dream custom house would be like?

"If it is a studio, tables and desks will come out. If it is a film house, a projection screen with benches and stools will come out. If it is a children's home, small furniture with cars, animals and a playground will come out," suggests Jurgen Bey.

House of Furniture

Studio Makkink & Bey

DESIGN / Studio Makkink & Bey
PHOTOGRAPHY / Nicoló Degiorgis
LOCATION / Milan, Italy

OVERVIEW was BIG-GAME's first solo exhibition in a museum. It took place at the Grand-Hornu Images in Belgium and the designers accompanied the project with a book published by Stichting Kunstboek called DESIGN OVERVIEW. The exhibition retraced BIG-GAME's industrial design work since 2004 and showed mostly prototypes. The scenography used simple pine wood plinths to create a context for the objects. The exhibition also showcased the photographic works that accompanied the design.

OVERVIEW
BIG-GAME

DESIGN / BIG-GAME
PHOTOGRAPHY / Michel Bonvin, Milo Keller
LOCATION / Belgium

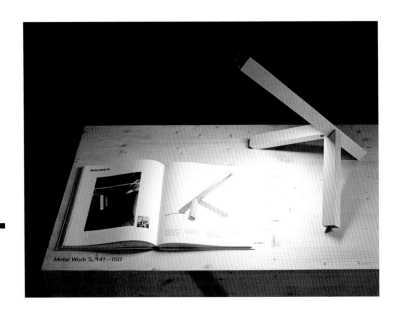

The graphic and exhibition design for the first major Japanese retrospective of internationally-known milliner Akio Hirata's seventy years of work. For the exhibition space, the designers wanted to make Hirata's hats stand out. The mass-produced non-woven fabric hats the designers created for the space are the antithesis of Hirata's carefully handmade hats, and bring them into sharp relief through dramatic contrast. Hirata oversaw the shape of these hats, which float and stream through the exhibition like ghosts or shells of the real hats exhibited. Some are exhibition stands; others become walls, ceilings and diffusers to scatter light through the space. Flooded with roughly 4000 of these 'ghost hats' as though shrouded in a cloud, the exhibition space softly invites visitors inside. There, they find no clear-cut paths to follow but an environment in which they can wander and discover Hirata's creations as they like, as a way of physically experiencing the creative freedom that underlies Hirata's work.

Akio Hirata's Exhibition of Hats
Nendo

DESIGN / Nendo
PHOTOGRAPHY / Nendo
LOCATION / Japan

Overtreders W designed shipping containers out of textiles for the exhibition Portscapes at Museum Boijmans van Beuningen, Rotterdam.

The exhibition Portscapes is the culmination of a year-long cultural project that invited Dutch and international artists to reflect on Maasvlakte 2, the extension of Rotterdam's harbour. Underway since 2008, the extension will increase Europe's largest harbour by 20%, enlarging The Netherlands by 2000 hectares. The resultant artworks include photography, performance, videos, sound installations and even a newspaper.

For the design of the exhibition, Overtreders W looked to the harbour for inspiration. The concept was to create a physical intervention in the space (Richard Serra Hall) as a basis for the artworks, many of which include visuals and sound. Shipping containers, iconic symbols of the harbour, are fashioned out of fabric to provide an intimate backdrop for experiencing each artwork. Constructed from textiles with differing transparencies – voile, cotton and cheesecloth – the containers paint an illusory image of the docklands in reference to a harbour that's not yet built. The textiles give a glimpse into the contents of the ubiquitous metal boxes which normally otherwise would remain a mystery. Texts for each artwork are printed onto cotton labels and stitched onto the containers. Through the play of transparencies - suggesting ships moving through a fog-filled harbour - the exhibition slowly reveals itself.

Connecting the different containers and artworks, rough textured black floor tiles- inspired by basalt tiles often found in harbours - guide visitors through the exhibition.

Portscapes
Overtreders W

DESIGN / Reinder Bakker & Hester van Dijk
PHOTOGRAPHY / Jorn van Eck
LOCATION / Rotterdam, the Netherlands

Richard Serra zaal
Richard Serra room

'18th-Century porcelain in contemporary architecture'

In the Netherlands, Meissen porcelain is often regarded as 'high-class kitsch'. Its sumptuous and narrative style of decoration puts it at odds with the minimalistic and conceptual traditions of Modernism. Solid Objectives – Idenburg Liu (SO-IL) was commissioned by Kunsthal KAdE to design an ideal contemporary three-dimensional setting in which to present the porcelain so that it would challenge this prejudice and focus attention on the great sculptural, artistic and technical strengths of Meissen. In response, SO-IL has designed 32 modern, geometrically shaped showcases in bright colors and with 'pointed tops'. These showcases not only serve the Meissen objects but are also autonomous in character. The designers wanted to devise a strategy that triggers the visitor to literally 'revisit' their initial understanding of the objects in the exhibition. By designing the cabinets not to 'display' but to actually 'dissect' the conventional viewing of the object, the visitor is forced to redefine his or her relationship to the work. The organization of color, shape and material decreases the individuality of pieces and their object-like character, to create a more fluid and visceral experience. It is a transition from object to experience, and shows architecture's potential to act as a mediator in this process.

Meissen I So – IL
Solid Objectives - Idenburg Liu

DESIGN / Florian Idenburg and Jing Liu
PHOTOGRAPHY / Iwan Baan
LOCATION / Amersfoort, the Netherlands

The design for an exhibition of 62 craft objects by 50 artisans at the 21st Century Museum of Contemporary Art, Kanazawa, in western Japan. The objects' materials range widely, including glass, wood, ceramics, metal and cloth. A variety of techniques were used in their creation, and they vary greatly in size. For the exhibition design, then, the designers chose the opposite strategy. Small mass-produced home-use greenhouses give a sense of order to the space and provide visitors with a flat perspective from which to view the exhibition, allowing the rich variety of the objects to stand out. The greenhouses also suggest the metaphor of the museum's hopes that crafts will continue to grow and flourish like plants.

The greenhouses are made completely of glass, and each comes with its own shelving and pre-installed wiring for lighting. They are inexpensive, perfect for small budgets, and are easily assembled with only a screwdriver. It took only one day to assemble all 62 of the boxes.

International KOGEI Triennale Pre-event

Nendo

DESIGN / Nendo
PHOTOGRAPHY / Nendo
LOCATION / Japan

This major retrospective on the works of Zaha Hadid Architects took place within the salone of Palazzo della Ragione, Padua, Italy. The exhibition examines the practice's continued experimentation and research into digital design and construction methods at the cutting edge of the industry.

The Salone of Palazzo della Ragione (constructed 1172-1219) is considered one of the most notable monuments in Padua. Its medieval roof remains amongst the largest in Europe unsupported by columns, while the frescoes that adorn the interior walls date from 1425. As with each of their projects, Zaha Hadid Architects have organized this exhibition as a direct response to the surrounding environment (in this case, within the salone), articulating the inherent contextual relationship of the work.

The historic qualities of the space presented an exacting design challenge for Zaha Hadid Architects. The exhibition design respects these spatial and contextual characteristics whilst also intervening in the unique manner of Hadid's digital, liquid fluidity. Space has been organized as a single fluid landscape with connecting individual fragments and clusters. A component system of hundreds of differentiated blocks swarms through the space of the Salone, allowing for both a large scale redefinition of the space and the minute display of detailed project information. The blocks vary in height reflecting and rebalancing the inverted roof of the Salone, giving it a completely new image yet respecting its integrity. On each block projects are displayed using a large variety of media such as: drawings, paintings, pictures, physical presentation and study models, prototypes and videos.

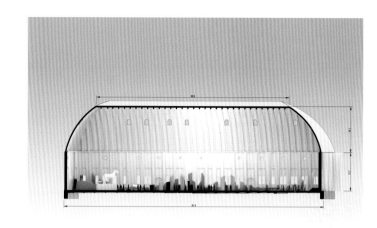

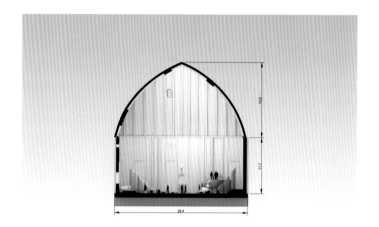

Zaha Hadid – PALAZZO DELLA RAGIONE PADOVA
Zaha Hadid Architects

DESIGN / Zaha Hadid Architects
PHOTOGRAPHY / Fabrizio Marchesi
LOCATION / Padua, Italy

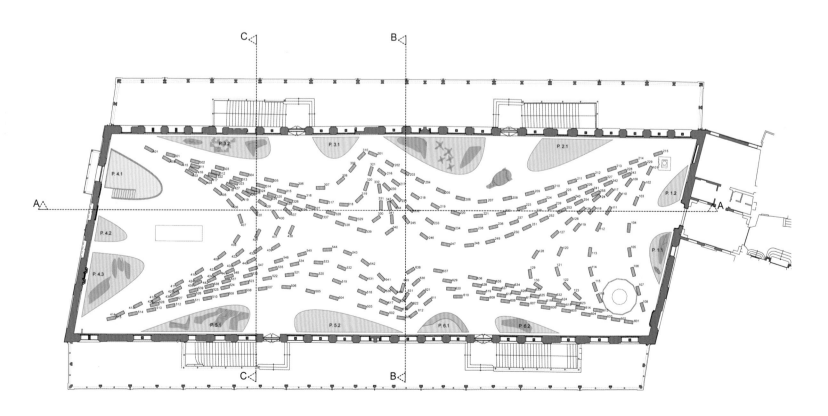

The More Trees Exhibition- Feeling the Forest for 12 Days was held at Axis Gallery in Roppongi, Tokyo. It aimed to introduce the activities of 'more trees' and reforestation projects, while new products made from thinned wood were exhibited. Two hundred of a selected products were hung throughout the exhibition space, and in the center of it the designers created a 4m wide round table made from thinned timber, on which the products were exhibited. The designers wanted to create a space where, as with taking a stroll in a forest, visitors can find their way through hanging branches while encountering new things.

More Trees Exhibition
- Feeling the Forest for 12 Days
TORAFU ARCHITECTS

DESIGN / TORAFU ARCHITECTS
PHOTOGRAPHY / Takumi Ota
LOCATION / Tokyo, Japan

Presented at the KAWASAKI CITY MUSEUM, "Yuichi Yokoyama - A complete record of Neo Manga: 'I am Depicting Time.'" is Yuichi Yokoyama's first exhibition. Yokoyama is an up-and-coming artist with a painting background who discovered manga as a form of expression that inspired him to create original works of art.

The site features an unpartitioned area covering 600m^2 where visitors can appreciate his early art works alongside a whole vast collection of story-boards from his most representative manga; New Engineering, Travel and NIWA. The museum's characteristic curved wall inspired the designers to create a track-and-field-like exhibition space where visitors complete laps by following the drawings placed along the inner and outer rings. Japanese manga reads from right to left, conducting visitors on the inside to move in the opposite direction from those on the outside. This setting allows them to view the same displays while ensuring they move past each other once, thus maintaining a feeling of distance. The semi-directive line of movement allows for a simplified route and selective movement to coexist on the same track.

The artificial lawn covering the exhibition floor accompanied by the dry brushing sound caused by footsteps resonates with the perspective on nature and sound-effects expressed in NIWA. Facing the screen at the center are benches made out of wooden crates and transport pallets owned by the museum, reminiscent of engineering structures.

Yuichi Yokoyama Solo Exhibition
TORAFU ARCHITECTS

DESIGN / TORAFU ARCHITECTS
PHOTOGRAPHY / Takumi Ota
LOCATION / Japan

The title "Hofer Wanted" already gives a hint that the exhibition on Tyrol's national hero is not a "glorification" but instead seeks to approach the historic figure differently. And the word "Wanted" indicates that a reward was announced for his head, as in Western movies when a thief or villain is on the run from the law. So what was it that Andreas Hofer was "guilty" of? And what kind of person does the exhibition try to portray? Within the scope of the anniversary of the 1809 Tyrolean rebellion, the first exhibition level comments on the contradictory character of Hofer the hero and scrutinizes popular perceptions, inviting visitors to actively explore the history themselves. The iconic qualities identified with a landlord, merchant, and heroic defender are set amidst an abstract architecture of narrative panels that suggest a mountain panorama and define the exhibition space in the shape of a complex sculpture. The second exhibition level, which focuses on Andreas Hofer the myth as well as the significance the rebellion had on the following 200 years after the event, leads through an open path of alternate angles and perspectives. The exhibits, boldly displayed in light pyramids to appear like "relics", are interspersed with topics that illuminate everyday culture back then. Together they show a multi-faceted picture offering visitors an exciting experience of the historic figure and his time.

Hofer Wanted
büromünzing 3d kommunikation

DESIGN / Dr. Claudia Sporer-Heis
PHOTOGRAPHY / brigida gonzález
LOCATION / Stuttgart, Germany

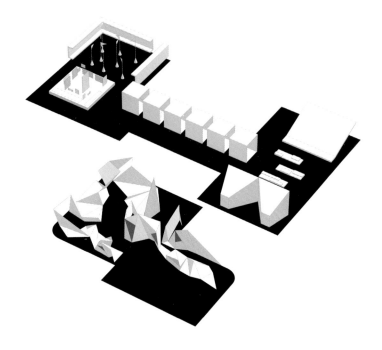

The installation Formations, developed by Matias del Campo and
Sandra Manninger specifically for the MAK Gallery in Vienna, is
based on the mathematical concept of recursive geometric systems
present in natural systems. These rigorous explorations conducted
within the office, with the goal of finding novel opportunities
for the articulation of architectural bodies, based on similarity
and continuous growth. The mathematical background for this
exploration was formulated by the mathematician Benoit Mandelbrot,
and includes the application of algorithms.

The installation is not supposed to represent a metaphoric
approach to natural phenomena, but is instead intended as a
research setting for organic sensibilities and their effect on
space. The rigorously applied formula consists of two fundamental
architectural qualities: geometry and repetition. These two
elements form the core of the design strategy for the installation.

Formations Exhibition MAK Vienna
SPAN/del Campo, Manninger

DESIGN / SPAN/del Campo, Manninger
PHOTOGRAPHY / SPAN/MAK
LOCATION / Travelling Exhibition

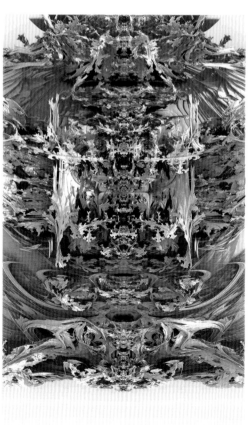

The Cairo pods asked the designers to explore opportunities within the aggregation of repetitive objects that imply the creation of heterogeneous figurations. The Cairo Tessellation, known in mathematics also as equilateral Pentagons that tile the plane, allows for a high variety of the topology of the plane. In the case of the Cairo pods the designers extended the plane in the third dimension and delaminated specific elements emerging out of the basic planar geometry to form three elements to comprise one pod. The pod's purpose is to serve as exhibition vitrine in varying spaces. The Tessellation allows the designers to aggregate the repetitive component in multiple ways, to adapt to different exhibition environments without compromising the overall appearance of the design.

Exhibition design commissioned by the Az W (Architecture Center Vienna) for the exhibition Housing in Vienna.

Formations – HOUSING IN VIENNA
SPAN/del Campo, Manninger

DESIGN / SPAN/del Campo, Manninger
PHOTOGRAPHY / SPAN/HOUSING IN VIENNA
LOCATION / Travelling Exhibition

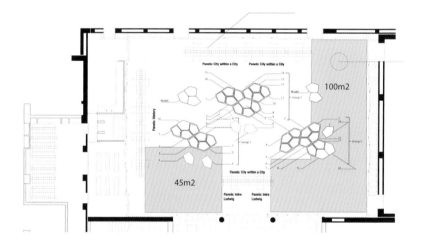

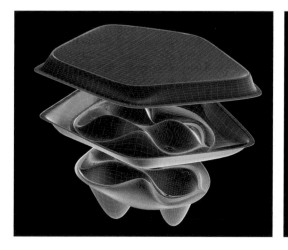

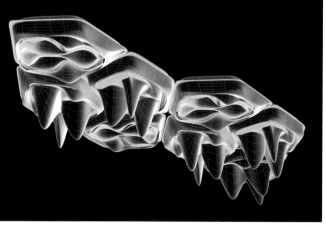

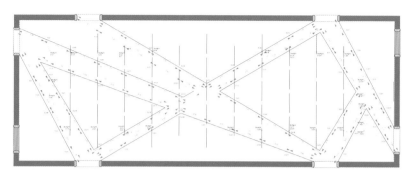

Enclosures Plan _ Anchor Points Distribution _ Banners

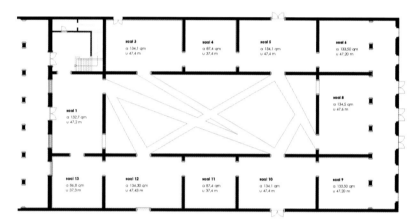

traditional pattern

black and white

pixelate

patch

original textile

woven pattern

horizontal stretch

vertical stretch

APPLIED DIGITAL PROCESS

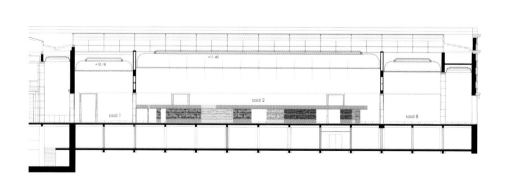

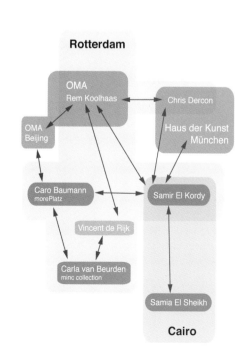

The project aims to scale the space to the object that will be displayed, providing order and rhythm to an exhibition that wants to be intimate. The models of public sculptures done by Susana Solano are treated as jewels that relate to each other visually as well as historically.

A single system is designed to suit two spaces with opposed spatial attributes, allowing for a single reading of the exhibit. A unique envelope sought to unify spatial perception while solving by its layout the display of the pieces.

A fragile, translucent, white, almost sacramental envelope is built to receive a number of sturdy and powerful pieces. The reference is clear: the paper lamp form used in fairs, made out of a fragile honey comb paper, with its volume built up from air bubbles and inventiveness. The project reflects a desire in the paper industry to find a material that will fulfill architectural aims will still being ecologically friendly and economical.

The installation not only responds to ecological and sustainable issues but also uses a material created out of recycled paper which can be used again. The decision to use this material radically decreased the overall project cost.

Susana Solano Exhibition

Cadaval & Solà-Morales

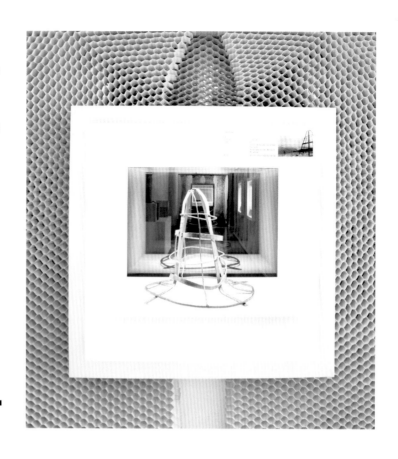

DESIGN / Eduardo Cadaval & Clara Solà-Morales
PHOTOGRAPHY / Adrià Goula, Santiago Garcés, Manolo Iyera
LOCATION / Spain

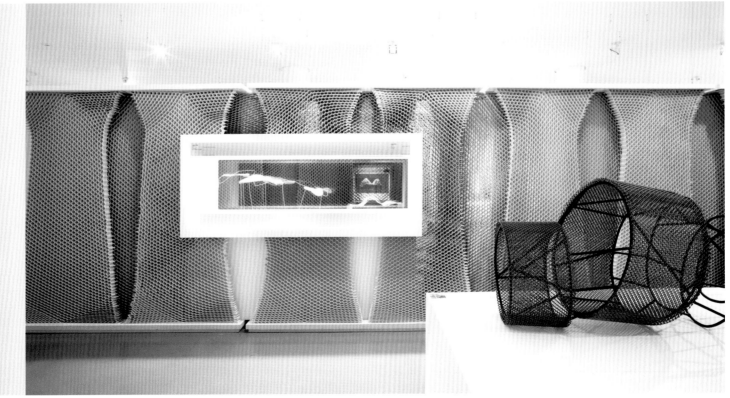

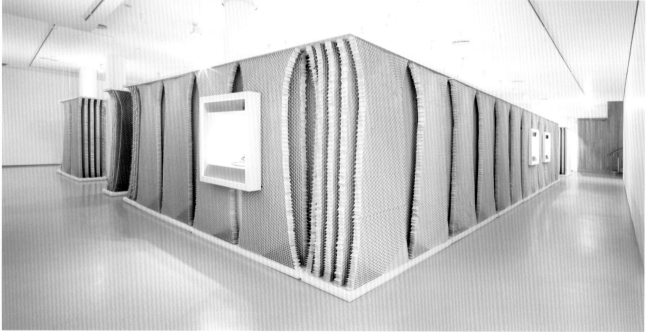

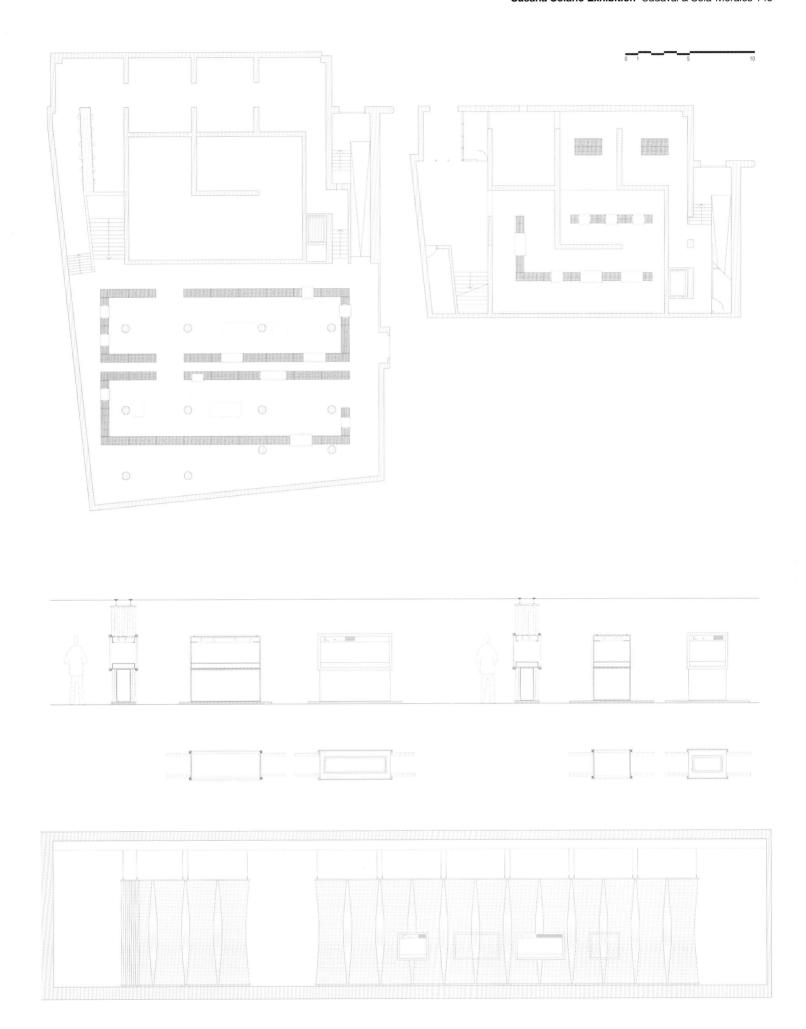

The Exhibition "bones" was designed as "Exhibition 5" (the fifth exhibition) of 21_21 DESIGN SIGHT. This exhibition, directed by Shunji Yamanaka, directs the designers' attention to the relationship between function and form in industrial products, while considering the sophisticated structures of the bones of living things.

The exhibition is comprised of two parts: "Specimen Room" and "Laboratory." The former possesses samples of "bones" of living things and industrial products while the latter introduces the works that were created to explore "the bones of the future." Since the showpieces in "Specimen Room" are relatively smaller objects such as precision apparatus, they are exhibited in a Z-shaped corridor. Contrary to the usual flow planning, the designers located the "Laboratory" in front of this narrow "Specimen Room" with a view toward providing a sense of extensiveness of the future.

The exhibition site is thickly forested with columns and when visitors look into this forest, they will catch glimpses of the various exhibition pieces. The columns that seem to have been randomly placed within this space gently partition off each exhibit and at the same time invite visitors to move about freely to examine each piece up close.

Exhibition "bones"

TORAFU ARCHITECTS

DESIGN / TORAFU ARCHITECTS
PHOTOGRAPHY / Masaya Yoshimura
LOCATION / Tokyo, Japan

This is the second part of a charity art exhibition held by the National Federation of UNESCO Associations in Japan to promote World Heritage related activities. The event entitled "PIECE of PEACE - World Heritage Exhibit Built with Lego" opened at Shibuya's PARCO store before departing on a nation-wide tour.

The circular tables of varying sizes on which the Lego exhibits are presented come together seamlessly like a string of beads in any configuration regardless of the exhibition space available. The designers sought to bring out the vivid colors and jagged contours of the Lego blocks with the help of a spotlight by dramatizing the contrast between the works standing on a perfectly white circle and the surrounding floor and walls covered in black.

PIECE of PEACE - World Heritage Exhibit Built with Lego
TORAFU ARCHITECTS

DESIGN / TORAFU ARCHITECTS
PHOTOGRAPHY / Takumi Ota
LOCATION / Tokyo, Japan

The architects designed the venue for the "Happiness is SNOOPY - Snoopy's Pursuit of a Piece of Happiness Exhibition" that was held at Ikebukuro Sunshine City in Tokyo.

For this exhibition, the designers proposed a site where every corner is made up of the scattered pages of a picture book titled "Happiness is a Warm Puppy".

The panels have different graphics on each side, and each corner is delimited by panels of the same color. Visitors experience its contents by moving through the site as the colors that fill the spaces around them change, like flipping through the pages of a book.

The front and back of the panels have been built to come apart at the end of the exhibition. That way the layout of the exhibition pieces can be altered at each stop during a nationwide tour.

By bringing the original graphics into play and adopting simple and flat content, visitors are given the feeling of stepping into a picture book.

The designers envisioned an exhibition where everyone is free to explore the site and discover, as the theme suggests, a "Piece of Happiness" to bring back home.

Happiness is SNOOPY
- Snoopy's Pursuit of a Piece of
Happiness Exhibition
TORAFU ARCHITECTS

DESIGN / TORAFU ARCHITECTS
PHOTOGRAPHY / Daici Ano
LOCATION / Tokyo, Japan

MVRDV, The Why Factory and the JUT Foundation for Arts and Architecture opened the fourth edition of the exhibition series "Museum of Tomorrow" in Taipei, China. Under the title "The Vertical Village" the exhibition explores the rapid urban transformation in East Asia, the qualities of urban villages and the potential to realize ideal spaces in a much denser, more vertical way as a radical alternative to the identical block architecture with standard apartments and its consequences for the city. The exhibition consists of analytical research, a grid of models, various movies, a documentary and animations, two software packages and a 6-meter tall installation of a possible Vertical Village developed by MVRDV and The Why Factory. Visitors can design their ideal house and compose their own Vertical Village with parametric software. The exhibition is located in Chung Shan Creative Hub, Taipei, China and is open until January 2012.

Vertical Village

MVRDV

DESIGN / MVRDV + The Why Factory
PHOTOGRAPHY / Zoe Yeh
LOCATION / Taiwan, China

Black was invited by Design Singapore Council to conceptualize, curate & design the landmark exhibition, 20/20. It was an ongoing showcase of Singapore's finest design talents, charting the paradigm shift that has occurred within Singapore's creative landscape. The exhibition featured scaffolding and an industrial conveyor belt inspired by the theme of Singapore's design industry being under construction.

20/20 Under Construction
Black Design

DESIGN / Jackson Tan
PHOTOGRAPHY / Black Design
LOCATION / Singapore

The subjects of McCurry's photographs represent the reality hidden behind glossy printed communication forms which pretend to represent humanity. And so, as Mandelbrot has provided the first mathematical tools to deal with the chaos, McCurry provides the audiences with visual accounts that explore diversity. Steve has all the characteristics of the true researcher: from the patience necessary to carry out an experiment (or to take a photograph), to the restlessness that always pushes him toward a new frontier to cross. The designer tried to represent, within the large spaces of the Macro, a layout similar to a nomad's village with structures that merge to restore a sense of solidarity. The exhibition project does not consider spatial-temporal variables but instead works on the assonance of subjects and unexpected degrees of kinship that restore a sense of humanity. There is life and death in McCurry's photos, and that short or long itinerary that links them; like the way and the sense itself of this exhibition that will lead the visitors to be nomads by choice, pioneers out of need.

Steve McCurry

Studio Fabio Novembre

DESIGN / Patrizio Mozzicafreddo, Alessio Scalabrini
PHOTOGRAPHY / Pasquale Formisano
LOCATION / Rome, Italy

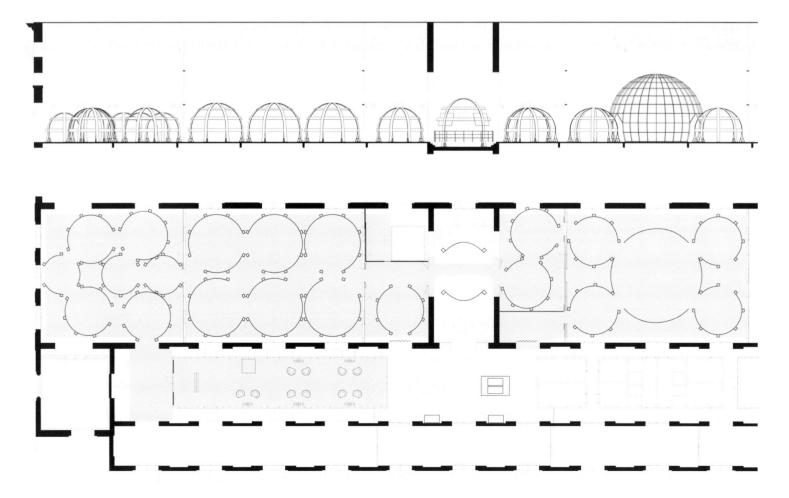

The Australian Racing Museum and Hall of Fame projects a sophisticated contemporary image that matches the bold architecture of its location at Federation Square and engages a new audience to marvel at the stories told. Sporting, social history and natural history themes are combined. The museum brings the world of racing to the attention of a new, young generation and allows them to experience something of the excitement and the glamour of the sport.

Exhibits include the skeleton of Carbine, the winner of the 1890 Melbourne Cup and one of Australia's greatest horses. Through the drama of digital visual effects and their integration with the exhibition spaces, new life is breathed into the objects, artefacts, and personalities of racing's history.

A feature of the museum is the way that conventional distinctions between exhibition design and architecture converge. The exhibition design and its architectural spaces are the outcome of close collaboration between emerystudio and Spowers Architects.

Australian Racing Museum
Emerystudio

DESIGN / Emerystudio
PHOTOGRAPHY / Emerystudio
LOCATION / Melbourne, Australia

Opened in May 2011, the Shanghai Museum of Glass represents not only a welcome addition to the city's cultural scene, but also an exciting milestone in the relentless renewal and regeneration of China's financial capital.

From the gleaming façades of myriad skyscrapers, to historical ties with international craftsmanship and style, to recently unearthed archaeological gems, Shanghai's mastery of glass is as long as it is versatile. Fittingly housed in the former premises of the Shanghai Glass Factory, the museum pays homage to this extensive history, skill and indeed very fabric of Shanghai today, where swathes of glistening glass-clad towers dominate the cityscape.

Coordination Asia were approached by Zhang Lin, the museum's CEO, and, guided by his sheer passion for the beauty and almost limitless potential of glass, created a showcase that inspires, educates and intrigues. Taking leads from a portfolio of successful projects completed internationally, Coordination's design and concept has set a new standard for Shanghai museums.

Interactive in approach, the museum includes exhibits that incorporate technology and consider presentation and visitor engagement. Digital displays describe the molecular makeup of glass through easy-to-understand graphics that guide visitors through the galleries. The history of glass in China and abroad is accentuated with beautifully lit artifacts that use the material's unique qualities to achieve spectacular effects. Younger museum-goers can discover the many applications of glass through fun installations, whilst a ceiling-high LED screen bridges the museum's various areas, its lights glistening in display cases and artworks.

Shanghai Museum of Glass

COORDINATION ASIA Architecture Design
Consulting Co., Ltd

DESIGN / Tilman Thürmer
PHOTOGRAPHY / diephotodesigner.de, Berlin/Germany
LOCATION / Shanghai, China

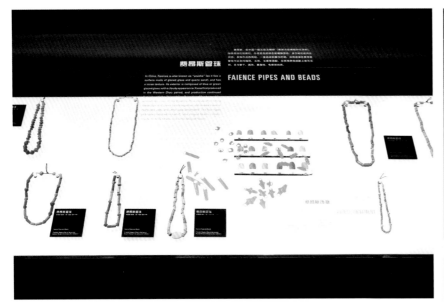

The exhibition design for the 'Japan: Tradition. Innovation' exhibition at the Canadian Museum of Civilization. The exhibition, which is divided into five sections devoted respectively to transportation, robotic technology, social status, consumer culture and play, uses a comparison between contemporary artwork and artwork of the Edo Period (1615-1868) in Japan to explore and interpret the relationship between Japanese culture and design. Given the massive 970m^2 space, the designers decided to use 'roofs' in a variety of sizes and heights to demarcate the different exhibits, rather than constructing temporary interior walls. A subway map-like graphic on the floor allows visitors to identify the different zones. Areas under larger, lower roofs are 'closed' spaces, and the light that falls between the many smaller roofs like sunbeams filtering through leaves creates a 'half-outdoor' space. Visitors look out into 'outside spaces' from underneath the roofs and -conversely- peer back into 'inside spaces', producing a hybrid, effervescently-changing space in which the relationship between inside and outside can never be known for sure. At first glance, clearly-defined lines of movement seem to have disappeared, and objects to be jumbled about in no visible order. However, in actuality the space is subtly, carefully divided using the invisible space-defining practices of 'ma' and 'shikiri', which have existed in Japan since ancient times. The result: the massive space loses its homogeneity, and provides visitors with the chaotic spatial experience of Japanese urban space.

Japan Tradition, Innovation, Canadian Museum of Civilization
Nendo

DESIGN / Nendo
PHOTOGRAPHY / Nendo
LOCATION / Canada

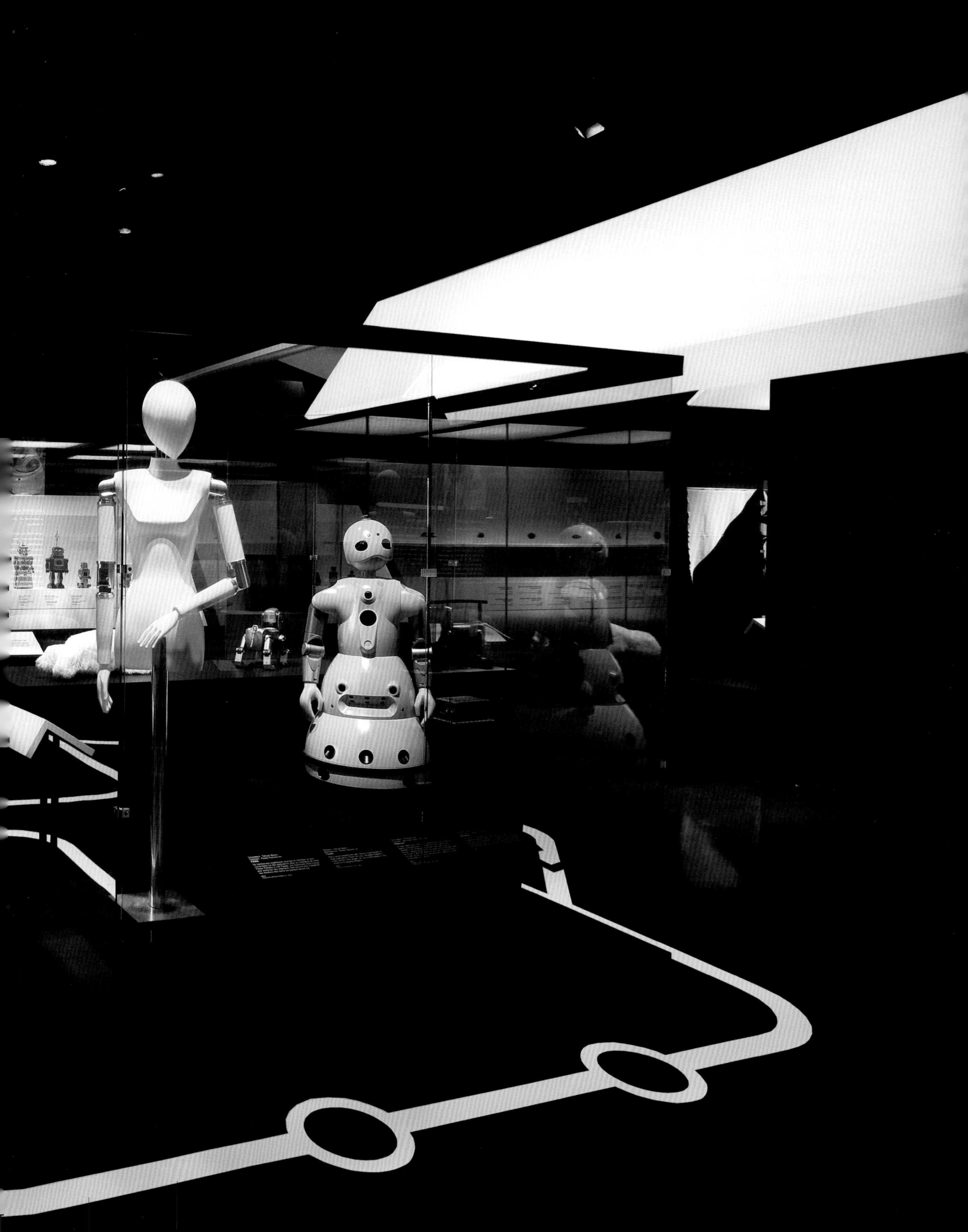

Beauty in Black is an intimate exhibition featuring 18 black-themed dresses from the 1950s to 2000s. They are part of the National Museum of Singapore's own collection, and come from renowned designers like Cristobal Balenciagia, Rei Kawakubo, Karl Lagerfeld, and local names such as Benny Ong and Thomas Wee.

The design takes its spin from a fashion runway show where the surrounding area is always quite dark, and attention is focused on the models and clothes. The designers wanted to explore a variety of finishes and materials for the space that are also 'softer' in nature, which alludes to the dresses, and which have various textures – like fabric, carpet, felt etc.

A central fabric platform is created as a distinctive feature to draw together all 18 different dresses. By doing so, it also allows one to walk around the dresses and take a closer view of them. The huge platform is lit from within, with all the captions printed directly onto it, each relating to the dresses suspended from above. From afar, it presents a mysterious vision of 18 intricate dresses floating dramatically over a huge lantern.

In addition, the designers have also created a black felt carpet wall that surrounds and wraps the space. Calling this a 'Black Ribbon', the wall extends outwards at the entrance, with its top gently curved to form a graceful collar, welcoming the visitor. The experience of this wall is not only visual, but textural too, as the other exhibition texts are printed directly on it, giving the words a sensual, haptic quality.

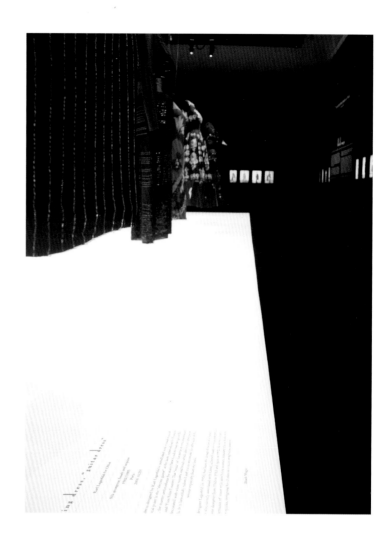

Beauty in Black

FARM

DESIGN / FARM
PHOTOGRAPHY / Jeremy San
LOCATION / Singapore

"Scheherazade is easy.
A little black dress is difficult"

the modern black dress

Before the 1900s, black was largely regarded in the West as the colour for mourning, despair and the sign of death and destruction. It was only popularly accepted as a colour symbolising fashion, modernity and productivity amongst women in the West from the 1920s.

Two major events — Britain's "Black Ascot" (1910) and the First World War (1914–1918) have been credited for changing the cultural status of black. The former referred to the royal racing event of 1910 which saw participants parading in black finery even as the nation mourned the death of King Edward II, hence raising the status of the colour black with luxury and *haute couture*. When war broke out in 1914, women adopted the wearing of the simple black mourning attire as a mark of economic conservatism and the need to be sensible and productive at war; the daily British newspaper, commented that this change was documented in both elite and the working class fashion publications by the 1920s which frequently portrayed models in black dresses and referred to them as fashionable, elegant and distinct.

the black dress in singapore

ck magic

nd
of the
ry,
colours
ed when
ess, black
igners

to
niques
nd
but
Ket,

there are others who relentlessly seek to present various shades of black by manipulating the effects created by light falling onto fabrics with different textures such as lace, velvet and wool.

In addition, designers also take advantage of light descending on monochrome black designs with embroidery and needlework to create eye-catching and three dimensional pieces, allowing the wearer to stand out in the crowd. For example, several pieces on display are elaborately embellished with sequins and beads to help break the austere look of black. Sometimes, colours are also employed to break the sombre mood of black. When black is combined with white (which reflects all colours), it also emphasises the graphic character of the outfit. Hence, despite the constant debate on black as a colour, the magical and sensory experience it produces in the form of the formal black dress should not be overlooked.

beauty in black

French couturier, Christian Dior (1905-1957), best described the appeal of black in a modern woman's wardrobe. "Black — the most popular and the most convenient and the most elegant of all colour. You can wear black at any time. You can wear it at any age. You may wear it on any occasion. I could write a book about black". Suitable for almost all occasions, black in fashion, in the guise of the "little" black dress, has been embraced by women all over the world since the early 20th century. Some of the most quoted reasons for wearing black are, it is versatile, easy to wear, elegant, respectable and understated. Black is often seen at black tie events, funerals and at work. It is also the "uniform" for some graduates, certain religious figures, professionals like lawyers and judges, classical musicians and subculture groups like Punk and Goth.

Beauty in Black attempts to examine why women and fashi general love black through a display of formal black dres the 1950s to the 2000s. The collection, on exhibit for the National Museum of Singapore, comprises purchases anc since 2004 and include creations by leading Western fashi Cristóbal Balenciaga, Hubert de Givenchy, Pierre Cardin, Karl Lagerfeld amongst others as well as Singaporean des Benny Ong and Thomas Wee. It also consists of garmen Singapore women during the 1950s and 1960s before rea popular in the 1970s. The sheer variety of fabrics, styles in these black dresses allow visitors to examine closely th skills of these selected designers.

There are three countries of the African continent in this exhibition, share several common traits - the Bantu language, the majestic Congo River and the great land of Africa herself. The land or the landscapes of Africa - from her dense and menacing rainforests to the stretches of the savannahs to the rapids of the river - have provided for and sustained these civilizations.

Because of this, the designers are inspired to create an abstracted and sinuous landscape that suggests the varied geography of these countries and thereby re-creating the contextual environment in which these artifacts are found and used.

A study of the various artifacts reveals similar characteristics amongst them -they are mostly figurines; they are not very large, and can be housed within a fixed dimension; and most of them will benefit from a 360 view all round to be studied in close-ups and details.

The designers wanted to ask if the method of display can be something more intrinsic and coherent to the whole spatial experience. The designers created plinths of various heights for the artifacts. They also serve as caption surfaces, seats, guide stands etc. As a design language, they form an organizational structure and logic to the space.

One circulates through the various sections of the exhibition in a linear fashion, although experientially, it is an organic and indirect one in which the visitor explores through a metaphorical landscape. They suggest, in parts, a forest, a meandering river, a hill, a temple, and a savannah grassland.

Congo River, Arts of Central Africa
FARM

DESIGN / FARM
PHOTOGRAPHY / Jeremy San
LOCATION / Singapore

The 'Box Mobile Gallery' responds to exhibition space needs. The gallery consists of 12 panels soft-hinged side by side. Each of these panels features an art work fixed to its inside. The flexibility of the soft hinge system enables spatial reconfiguration of the gallery, transforming one space into another according to site conditions, exhibition intention, and art media; from independent cells for an individual exhibition, to a common exhibition space for a group exhibition, often times with an introductory area or a courtyard and a special exhibition space for various art media.

The Box also functions as a crate. Art can be packed into the gallery, with some pieces sandwiched between panels and some contained within individual cells. In its folded and locked state, the box becomes an art crate, ready for travel or for storage.

When the Box Mobile Gallery encountered mobility art projects such as 'Mobility and Yi Sang's house drawings', as part of Yi Sang's house architectural program, the Box Mobile Gallery experimented with the idea that the territory of Yi Sang's house can be extended to its Tong-in Dong neighborhood, exhibiting a series of drawings of Yi Sang's house within.

After the first day of installation on the street at Yi Sang's house, the Box Mobile Gallery logged several days within an alley of local housing blocks, and then attracted street passengers at what was previously an outdoor parking lot under the PSPD building near Yi Sang's house. With this installation, people encountered an unexpected event in a city that created a renewed urban experience through the transformation of space.

Box Mobile Gallery
WISE Architecture

DESIGN / Young Chul Jang, Sook Hee Chun, Aram Yoon, Ji Soo Park
PHOTOGRAPHY / WISE Architecture
LOCATION / Seoul, Korea

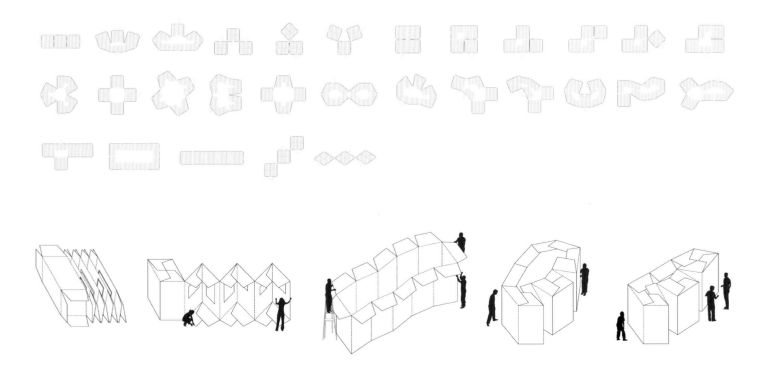

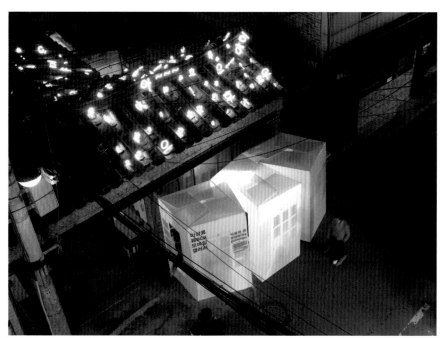

The Laboratory of Food Analysis is an interactive installation, developed by Maxime Morel and Lise Lefebvre. Designed as a playful critique of the basic approach of the diet and nutrition industry, the audience is encouraged to participate in a mock-scientific experiment. During the lab visit, visitors are assessed by a lab assistant who collects their physical attributes and personal data in order to manufacture a 'Nutricard'.

The Nutricard is a summary of their nutritional needs. It is made of edible paper soaked in different percentages of plant extracts according to the physiological information gathered during the consultation. For example, someone wearing glasses and who is tested to have a slightly elevated alkaline PH in their saliva will receive a personal Nutricard with a high percentage of carotene to improve eyesight and one printed with citrus extract to re-balance their PH.

The critique is based on simplistic analysis of nutritional data and the visitor's experience playfully draws attention to the process of diagnosis through only a short period of questioning and the prescribed treatment of only a small piece of edible paper.

Laboratory of Food Analysis

Lise LEFEBVRE & Maxime MOREL

DESIGN / Lise LEFEBVRE & Maxime MOREL
PHOTOGRAPHY / Maxime MOREL
LOCATION / Tokyo, Japan

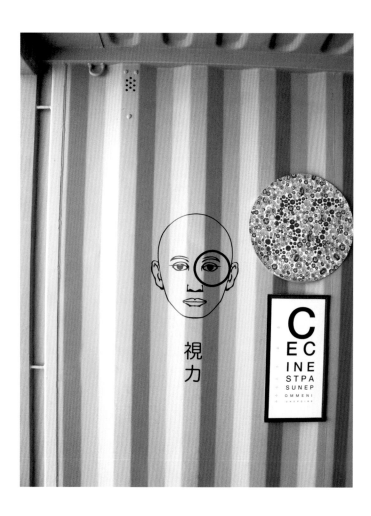

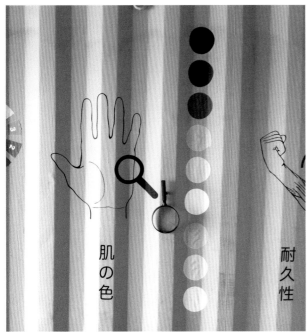

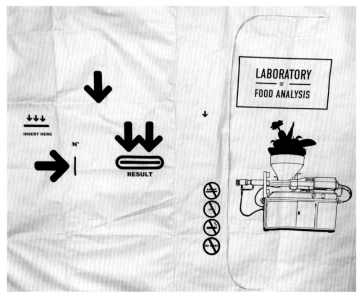

Conceived as an event space, Slowscape considers the speed of visitors' movements through the gallery and how the manipulation of built form can encourage us to pause and engage with the moving image. The intervention reworks the original gallery space to facilitate comfortable and intuitive forms of interaction.

A paneled timber structure gently rises across the rectilinear gallery at a canted angle, folding up to form a projection tower at the rear. From this point a platform wraps around existing columns and walls to form benches that engage otherwise overlooked areas in the open gallery space. The slight incline of the ramps encourages visitors to challenge the behavioral norms of the gallery by sitting or lounging on its surface.

Sixty lightweight recyclable stools were provided to complement the structure. Each was folded from a single cut sheet of fluted plastic and was designed to be placed in any position on the structure by compensating for the slope. This provision accommodated various formal events, film screenings, projections and discussions throughout the duration of the exhibit.

Shadowboxing Exhibition
Slowscape Collective

DESIGN / Stuart Franks, Christopher Kennedy, Ceri Williams and Thomas Woods
PHOTOGRAPHY / Stuart Franks, Ceri Williams
LOCATION / London, UK

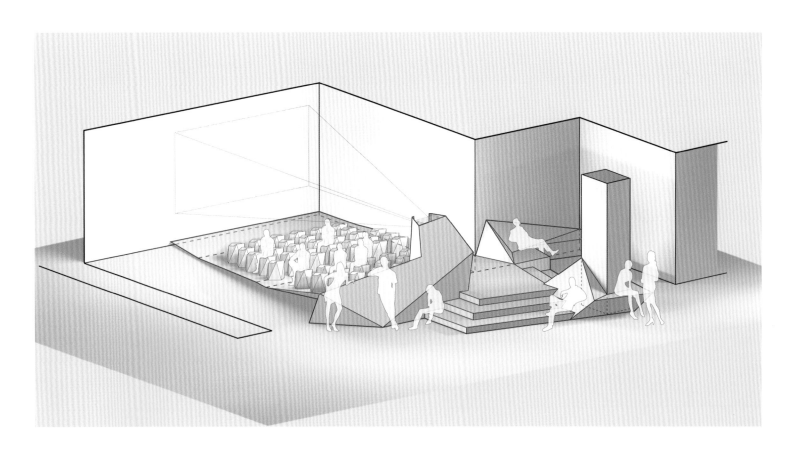

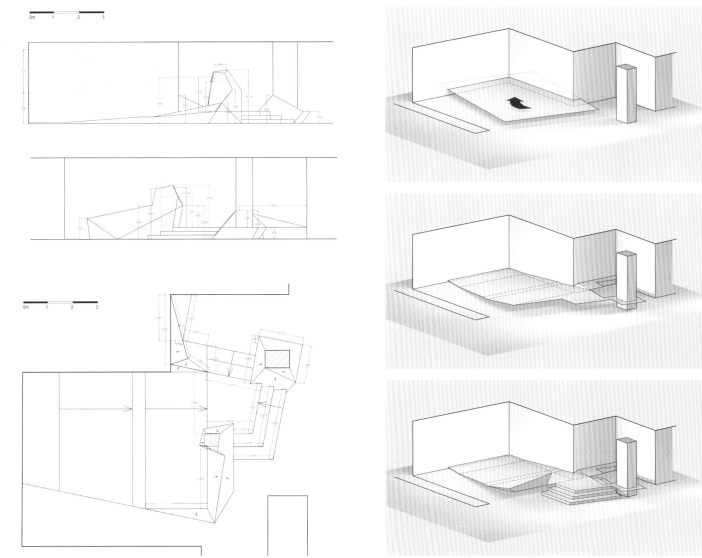

Jón Sigurðsson was always referred to as "president" in Iceland. The people of Iceland celebrate his birthday every year, as the National day of Iceland. The Republic of Iceland was also founded on his birthday on June 17th 1944. The exhibition is located on Sigurðsson's birthplace, Hrafnseyri by Arnarfjordur. Since 1980 there has been a small exhibition in Hrafnseyri but a committee appointed by the Prime Minister decided to hold a closed competition for a new exhibition on the life and work of Jon Sigurðsson to celebrate in 2010 the two hundred years anniversary of the birth of this Icon of the Icelandic liberation from the Danish State.

The proposal of Basalt Architects won the first prize as an innovative exciting solution. The core of the constructive idea is a 90-meter long continuous transparent wall of plexiglas that slides with smooth curves through all the rooms of the house. The story is told with different layers of pictures and texts; citing directly and indirectly the personal life of Jón Sigurðsson, the progression of the contemporary events and agents both in Iceland and abroad. Through his own reflection on the glossy coating of the plexiglas the visitor is constantly reminded of the fact that his reading of history is always relative to both time and placement. Interactive installations are incorporated in the exhibition; an interactive timeline on large touch-screens.

For the Good of the Nation
Basalt Architects

DESIGN / Basalt Architects
PHOTOGRAPHY / Sigridur Sigthorsdottir, Kristin Eva Olafsdottir, Johannes Long
LOCATION / Hrafnseyri, Iceland

Organized to coincide with Mercedes-Benz's 125-year anniversary, the exhibition provides a glimpse over the factory wall- right in the middle of the city of Sindelfingen. A former bank was converted to create this new exhibition space, which now also features a majestic staircase.

Spectacular large-scale exhibits fill the street-level display windows. Inside, visitors are greeted by a series of monitors showing Sindelfingen plant employees, inviting them to join the dialogue. Around 70 men and women were interviewed to create these engaging video clips, which provide personal insights into a variety of topics relating to automotive construction.

The Wissensband (Knowledge Wall) is a continuous series of wall-mounted display cabinets that seamlessly combines both exhibition levels. It presents a wide range of information in an anecdotal and playful manner, using text, photographs, drawings and exhibits.

The chronological Geschichtsband (History Wall) demonstrates how the history of the city and the factory are intimately bound. This history comes to life with the aid of a sliding monitor that allows visitors to select text, photos and videos.

In Werkspanorama (Factory Panorama), visitors can immerse themselves in the world of the Sindelfingen plant. The 360° display delivers a very special kind of cinematic experience: you can literally stand in the middle of the production process and watch the employees in action.

WerkStadt Dialog
jangled nerves

DESIGN / Thomas Hundt, Ingo Zirngibl with L2M3 Kommunikationsdesign
PHOTOGRAPHY / Axel Birnbaum, jangled nerves, L2M3
LOCATION / Sindelfingen, Germany

The exhibition SO100, presented during May to June at the zezeze architecture gallery, will present 100 works by architects Shahar Lulav and Oded Rozenkier, many of which have received various awards in Israel and internationally. The architects' unique works will be presented by utilizing a wide variety of media including physical models, renderings, films, drawings and plans.

The exhibition design creates an experience where the architects direct the visitor's viewing perception using free movement on mobile office chairs. The various exhibits occupy a three-dimensional grid above the viewer's head, and in an analogy to urban flaneury, the visitor experiences the exhibition in an unusual angle while moving about freely. Similarly to an urban excursion, the visitor may enter more intimate spaces where theme presentations of the architects' works are presented. Such themes include the handling of light, space, scenario, materiality, section, and other issues underlying their architectural work, receiving a unique and moving expression in the projects of Lulav and Rozenkier.

During the exhibition, the gallery will host a variety of open events. The planned events include a gala opening, talks by architects Lulav and Rozenkier, a talk by Yotam Bezalel Studio on commercial graphic branding, a talk on File to Factory techniques and demonstrations by RC-CG A, an event during the Houses From Within weekend and more.

SO100 Exhibition

SO Architecture

DESIGN / Shachar Lulv & Oded Rozenkier
PHOTOGRAPHY / Shai Epstein
LOCATION / Tel Aviv, Israel

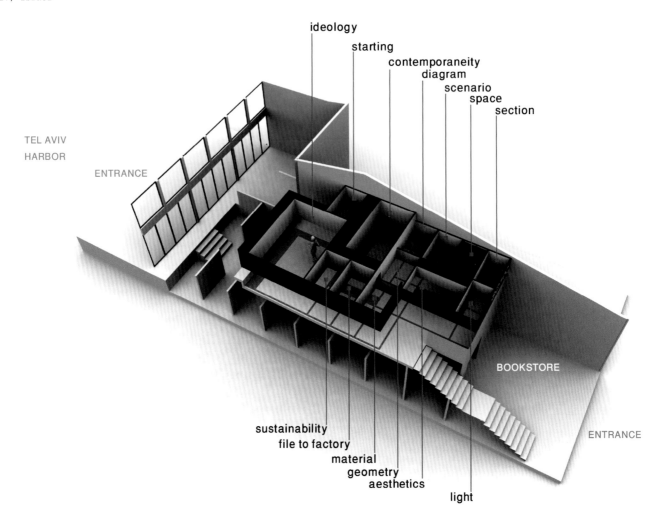

I am not telling the facts, I am relating stories. Are dreams or memories true?

What is born among the stupor of layers of asphalt and rays of sun? The flower is an abstraction, an idea of seduction, a fleeting moment between life and perfection with its petals and colors. We are bees to the scent, toasting with the nectar to dispense pollen.

At times you can confuse joy with pain, but then - "to do anything, you need a flower!"

Il Fiore di Novembre
Studio Fabio Novembre

DESIGN / Dino Cicchetti, Carlo Formisano
PHOTOGRAPHY / Pasquale Formisano
LOCATION / Milan, Italy

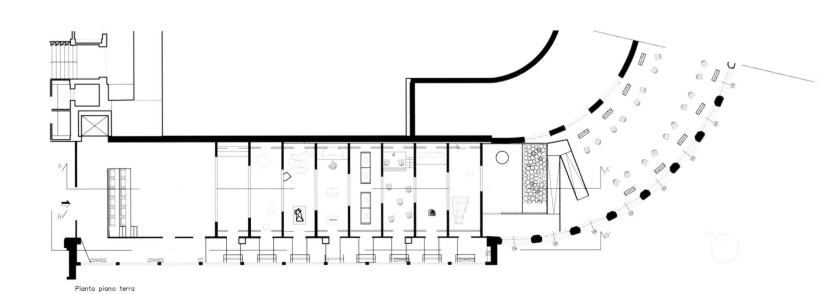

Pianta piano terra

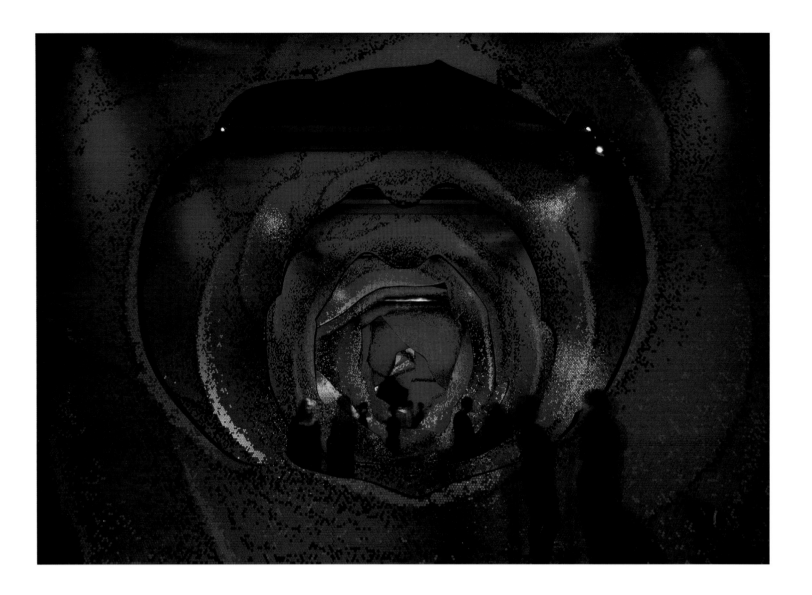

Sharing a passion for design, research, experimentation, aesthetic purity and technological innovation, BMW and Flos joined forces at Salone del Mobile 2011 to create, thanks to Paul Cocksedge's talent, SESTOSENSO, a celebration of light.

Inspired by the quality and beauty of light and the astonishing new BMW 6 Series, the first BMW with Full-LED headlights, Paul Cocksedge erected a seamless, curving, white wall extension to the Flos showroom and low-hanging red and white conical lamps. As with the BMW headlights, the source of light remains hidden, only the light itself is guided through a transparent body, rendering the light source invisible and forever changing its qualities.

Stepping inside one of the impressive SESTOSENSO red lights, a video of the BMW 6 Series Coupe reveals itself on the vast white wall. As if accessing a sixth sense, there is a hint of movement in the corner of the eye. Through the light the viewers see the car: through the car, they understand the light.

The playful sculptural pieces softly illuminate, stimulate and allow contemplation. Cocksedge gives us elegant, 'functional brilliance'.

SestoSenso for BMW & Flos

Paul Cocksedge Studio

DESIGN / Paul Cocksedge
PHOTOGRAPHY / Mark Cocksedge
LOCATION / Milan, Italy

The designers created the settings for the exhibition "Underground" which was held in Miraikan in Odaiba. The scale of this exhibition to bring "the underground" under review was one of the largest in Miraikan's history. The designers were required to make it possible for the visitors to deeply feel that the route starts from the earth surface and that it ends at the deepest part of the earth.

The designers proposed a stereoscopic method of display; the further visitors walked along the route, the higher the shielding blocks were piled. The large exhibition hall of 1600 square meters is composed of 6500 units of 500mm x 500mm x 400mm foamed styrene block. They used three kinds of styrene: 40% foamed, 50% foamed and 90% foamed. The lower level blocks consist of the heavier 40% foamed styrene and the higher level blocks consist of the lighter 90% foamed styrene. The white space covered with unitary module foamed styrene has a strong appeal and works as the background that flatters the showpieces. While there is the sensation of unity due to the use of this one simple material, the method of its use varies from a light fixture to a projection screen to signage.

Almost 100% of the foamed styrene is recyclable by dissolving after the exhibition. By using a material of a huge volume that can be easily processed, the designers finished setting the blocks in just one week.

Exhibition Underground

TORAFU ARCHITECTS

DESIGN / TORAFU ARCHITECTS
PHOTOGRAPHY / Daici Ano, TORAFU ARCHITECTS
LOCATION / Tokyo, Japan

What would a non-visual map look like? What would it feel like if you wandered within a forest of headphones, playing sounds from different places in Athens? How would you feel if you found yourself in a 'map' that only appeared when you walked in it?

In response to the main theme of the 11th Venice Biennale of Architecture ("Architecture Beyond Building"), the designers created an interactive sonic map of Athens, which presents in an unexpected way fragments of the atmosphere of the city. A forest of cables carrying hanging headphones creates a 'dense' environment, to be gradually explored.

This kind of sonic map is not an 'overview'; it is rather explored step-by-step by the visitor's movement. The encounter with the unexpected is part of the navigation, similar to the experience of the actual city. The visitor re-creates the space around him through his own presence and movement. The interactive environment of the pavilion space becomes a dynamic, changing field of multiple sonic qualities, layering and densities.

By magnifying the effects of human movement in space, ATHENS by SOUND brings forth the elusive sensuous aspects of space, such as sound, interaction, and atmosphere. A walk in the pavilion takes you 'out there', through invisible Athens.

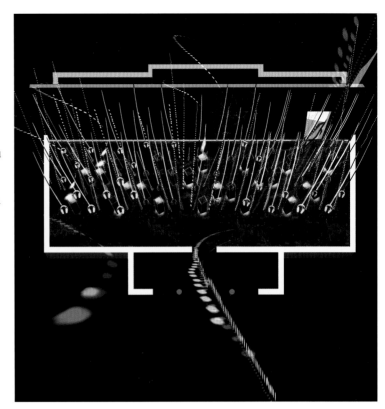

ATHENS by SOUND

Anastasia Karandinou, Christina Achtypi, Stylianos Giamarelos

---

DESIGN / Anastasia Karandinou, Christina Achtypi, Stylianos Giamarelos
PHOTOGRAPHY / Cathy Cunliffe
LOCATION / Venice, Italy

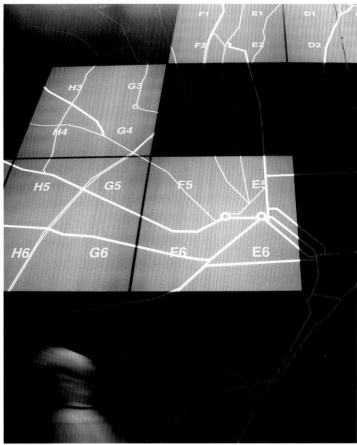

The exhibition frames Alex McDowell's original set designs for
films including Minority Report, Fight Club and Charlie and the
Chocolate Factory within his unique, non-linear production model—
the 'Matterball'. This graphic, 'the flavor tree machine' from
Charlie and the Chocolate Factory, and the circular exhibition
space, provide the conceptual starting point for this design.

In the center of the axially-composed space, stands a sculptural
spherical form. Manufactured through CNC milling using
contemporary digital techniques from the film industry, a robust
light-weight architecture is created. Inspired by View-Master
toys, the sphere's surface is radially punctuated with fourteen
view cones. Flat screen monitors embedded at differing heights
in the cones encourage a playful interaction with the audience.
Each station shows a film clip from a stage in the design process,
such as research, previs, or construction. By circulating around
the piece, viewers observe how the film design is developed,
culminating in a carved out interior lounge displaying the final
film extracts and a brief portrait/interview of Mr. McDowell.

Matterball Exhibition Sculpture at FMX

NAU

DESIGN / NAU
PHOTOGRAPHY / NAU
LOCATION / Stuttgart, Germany

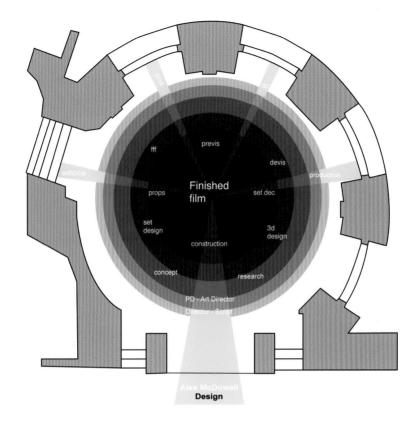

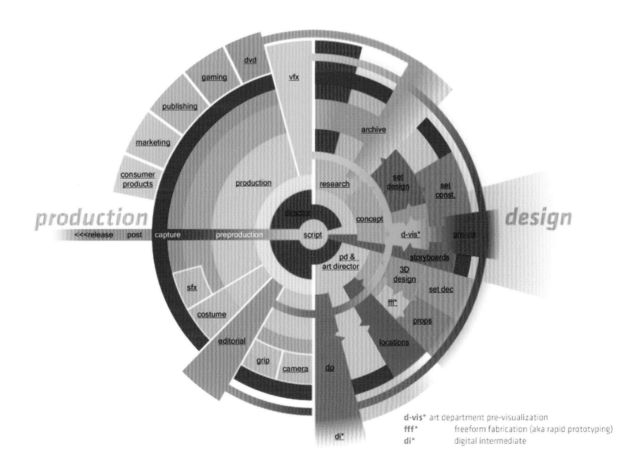

d-vis* art department pre-visualization
fff* freeform fabrication (aka rapid prototyping)
di* digital intermediate

Inaugurated on the occasion of the conference ACADIA 2010 LIFE information, the exhibition Evolutive Means examines concepts, tools and technologies that implement responsive and generative aspects of information in the design process.

In order to populate the exhibition layout, the compiled keyword list was anchored in the gallery space according to relationships specified by the curators. The intervention by the curator intentionally promotes curatorial critique through the exploration of possible relationships in a dynamic, fluid environment provided by the computational algorithm. Individual projects, however, are located based on their relationship to the keywords and other projects through a computational process of self-organization. The quantitative and qualitative keyword attributes provide the magnitude of the attraction and repulsion forces between the projects and the compiled keywords, determining the location of the individual projects in the gallery space as well as the attributes of the display volumes suspended from the ceiling.

The exhibition design utilizes a computation procedure that crowdsources the ACADIA community to uncover patterns of information that can be used to generate knowledge about contemporary technological issues. The objective of this pioneering protocol is to index the position of contemporary architectural ideas and concepts in relation to peer-reviewed projects, guest projects and the larger ACADIA community.

Evolutive Means
Open Source Architecture R&D

DESIGN / Chandler Ahrens, John Carpenter, Axel Schmitzberger and Michael W. Su
PHOTOGRAPHY / Courtesy of Open Source Architecture
Exhibition Curators / Chandler Ahrens (Open Source Architecture), Axel Schmitzberger, Michael W. Su, Pablo Lorenzo-Eiroa, Aaron Sprecher (Open Source Architecture) and Shai Yeshayahu
LOCATION / New York, USA

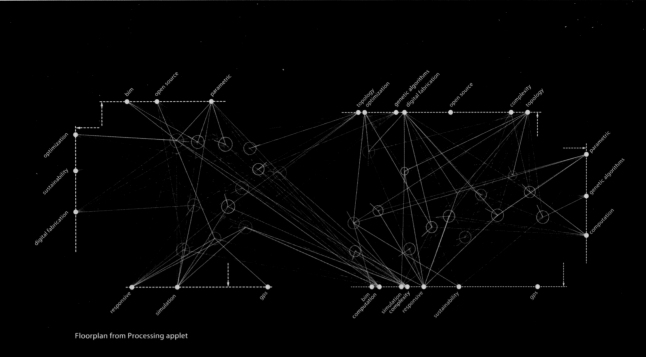

Floorplan from Processing applet

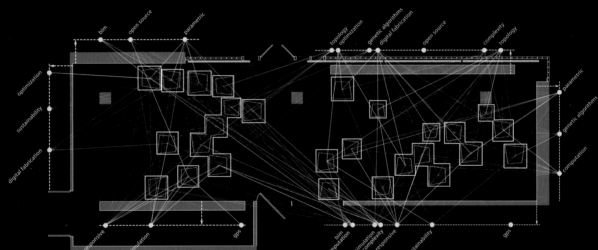

Floorplan of project cones, keywords and relational connecting lines

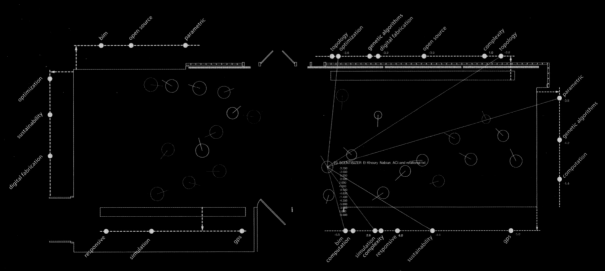

Floorplan of project data from Processing applet

Environment, society, economy: Level Green - The idea of sustainability, brings in the Autostadt in Wolfsburg these three dimensions together in a very unique way. The focus is on how we can protect our environment and preserve it for future generations. A wealth of information presented in interactive formats addresses the different aspects of sustainability and conveys knowledge on a spontaneous, sensory level.

The 1,000 square meters permanent exhibition opened in June 2009 and is divided into six themed areas with 25 hands-on displays. Visitors choose from different starting points and decide for themselves how deeply they want to explore a given topic. They are invited to become actively involved in the various themes and discover new ways of contributing to sustainable development in their daily lives.

Touch-sensitive data sculptures visualize facts and figures, making them more understandable and allowing for direct comparisons. Interactive media walls shed light on complex themes and encourage reflection on one's own lifestyle and habits. The idea is to evoke answers to questions on sustainability and create a personal connection to the issues.

Level Green Exhibition
– The idea of sustainability

J. MAYER H Architects

DESIGN / J. MAYER H Architects
PHOTOGRAPHY / Uwe Walter / Autostadt
LOCATION / Wolfsburg, Germany

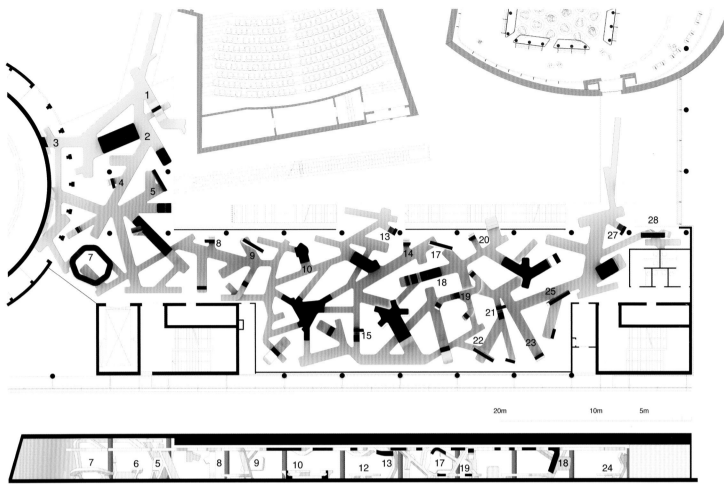

20m   10m   5m

1 Haupteingang **2** Virtuelles Wasser **3** Wandvorlage 360° Kino **4** Verbrauch im Vergleich **5** Ökologischer Rucksack **6** Ökologischer Fußabdruck **7** Automotive Lifecycle **8** Nachhaltigkeit bei Volkswagen **9** Antriebs- und Kraftstoffstrategien **10** interaktive Stausimulation **11** Idee der Nachhaltigkeit **12** Mobilitätsprofile **13** Eingang Mitte **14** Mobilität der Zukunft **15** Gesellschaftliche Verantwortung **16** Brunnen der Erkenntnis **17** Utopientester **18** Exponat Klimawechselwirkungen **19** Klimazeiten **20** Bereichkennzeichnung Klimawechselwirkungen **21** Nachhaltigkeit und Ökonomie **22** nachhaltig Wirtschaften **23** Talking Head **24** Klimatexturen **25** Medienwand Klimawechselwirkungen **26** CO^2-Einsparpotentiale **27** Eingang Mobiglobe **28** Medienecke

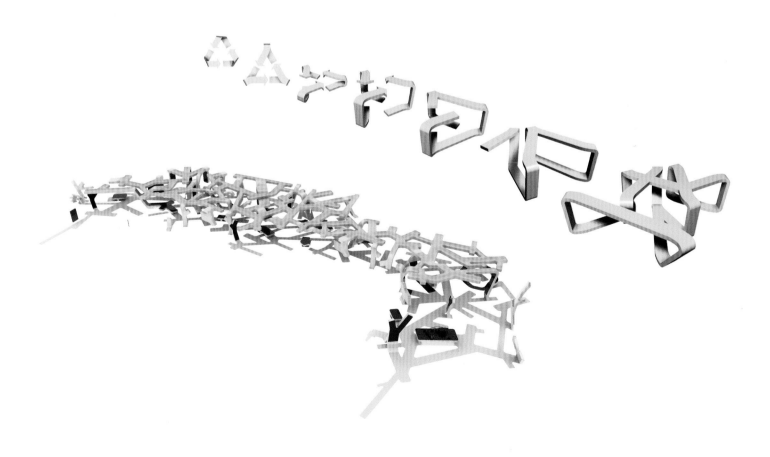

The designers were commissioned to design the new FC Barcelona museum. Their project for the new FC Barcelona museum was based on developing all the required capabilities to transport visitors to a landscape of emotions. The designers wanted the visit to be perceived as an experience of transportation to those particular and private moments that they all keep in their minds. Different languages should be able to cohabitate: objects and tradition + new media and innovative expressions. A space for knowledge and information, and a space for emotions and celebration.

New FC Barcelona Museum
EXITDESIGN

DESIGN / EXITDESIGN
PHOTOGRAPHY / EXITDESIGN
LOCATION / Barcelona, Spain

The exhibition presents twelve stories that explore the
space between design and science. The projects speculate on
possibilities of modification of the human body and the role that
designers may play in the process of dealing with the issues that
biology hasn't addressed yet. Mobile mini-devices, temporary
prostheses and active implants are designers' response to the
technological change. The projects form a powerful commentary on
contemporariness – our lifestyle, ambitions and desires. Some of
them go even further, developing speculative scenarios of what
may happen in the foreseeable future. They disturb our comfort
of being a user, making us wonder if what we witness is design
fiction or another step in the technological evolution.

The exhibition design aimed to create a notion of a workshop,
laboratory with a mood board-style setting where everything has
still to be decided. The narrative has been evolved around the
visual and verbal research across various disciplines that have
been accompanied by truly realistic videos and prototypes working
as testimonies of the future situations. The exhibition has been
developed in partnership with the British Council.

Design Faction

Kasia Jezowska

DESIGN / Kasia Jezowska
PHOTOGRAPHY / Maya Art, Piotr Chlipalski
LOCATION / Lodz, Poland

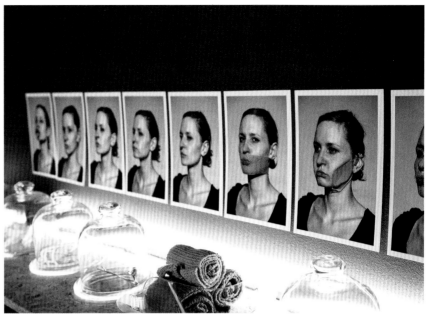

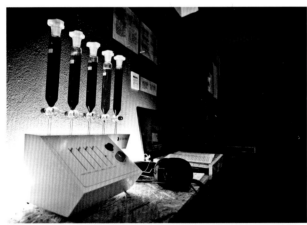

This is Universal Design Studio's third Wildlife Photographer of the Year exhibition design for the Natural History Museum. The exhibition showcases over 100 large, back illuminated photographs from a competition which is held annually by the museum. The 2011 competition attracted over 43,000 entries from 94 countries.

Situated within one of the magnificent Waterhouse galleries, Universal's concept was to inhabit the vast space with a contrasting light weight architecture of shadow. By using black, grey & white fabric scrim to form smaller, more intimate spaces, Universal has created an experience of shifting transparency and opacity, shadow and light, to poetically reinforce the photographic contents on show.

The 3 youth categories are located on the perimeter walls of the gallery and are outlined by a running floor light of deep Klein blue at low level. The line of blue is easily visible through the multiple layers of black scrim and helps to delineate the edges of the gallery. The perimeter walls are also clad in a sound absorbing wood wool material which subtly reinforces the exhibition's mysterious quality.

6m high and running lengthwise through the gallery space, the main scrim wall creates a dramatic transparent facade, with individual openings formed for each of the exhibition sections. Vertical lines of light punctuate the scrim and throw light onto its surface, creating areas of opacity.

Wildlife Photographer of the Year Exhibition 2011
Universal Design Studio

DESIGN / Universal Design Studio
PHOTOGRAPHY / Leon Chew
LOCATION / London, UK

The approach to the Pavilion of Portugal is marked by the presence of an enigmatic and symbolic facade. More than just decoration of the facade of the pavilion, a three meter high transparency was created of a matrix image of watersheds of three international rivers. This option controls the entry of natural light in the different halls of the pavilion, reducing energy consumption significantly.

The first moment of exposure, which is called the "Alert", develops into a tubular space, where the presence of projected images associated with mirrored surfaces and irregular geometries carries the one time visitors to "limit scenarios," warning of the real problems that cause climate changes. The great room of the exhibition refers to the second stage called "Conscience". The pavement / route is slightly raised over the existing pavement (20cm) and covers only the space needed for the exhibition route, leaving the areas to build not necessary, emphasizing the movement / flow of the river and at the same time calling attention to the relationship between essential and superfluous, criticizing waste. The third room, called "Change", seeks to project the visitors to a better future, but basically it means that each of us is the future.

The space was designed "Portugal Compartilha" in order to be visible to the outside and receive natural light through the facade, thus minimizing energy consumption.

Portugal Pavilion – Expo Zaragoza
Bak Gordon Arquitectos

DESIGN / Ricardo Bak Gordon
PHOTOGRAPHY / Fernando Guerra & Sérgio Guerra
LOCATION / Zaragoza, Spain

A hall is bathed in the deep, red and warm light of numerous heat lamps mounted on the ceiling. This is not the gate of hell, but a porch to life. It is a start for transformation. Through this installation, the visitors enter the world of 37.6 degrees Celsius/99.7 degrees Fahrenheit. This is exactly the temperature needed for an egg in a three-dimensional incubator to hatch.

At the end of the hall the visitor is drawn into a large room. An instructional video is explaining the crossbreeding Cosmopolitan Chicken Project of artist Koen Vanmechelen and prepares the visitor for the experience to come. On one side a large bird cage is looming, filled with tropical plants and the almost mythical Red Junglefowl, the ancestor of the domestic chicken. To access this cage, to enjoy a multisensory experience and walk the narrow line dividing the wild and the domestic, visitors must be disinfected: they are obliged to wear plastic shoes and a mouth mask. In the pre-human world of the Red Junglefowl, no human contamination or germs is allowed.

In the rest of the room ventilators are 'working' above 15 tables, which are presented as beds. Each and every one of them is nurturing a certain number of chicken eggs and symbolizes one of the 15 generations of chickens belonging to the Cosmopolitan Chicken Project. This is the artist's bicultural potential for transformation. These are the tools for the future.

'Modified Spaces – C.C.P'
The Cosmopolitan Chicken

DESIGN / Koen Vanmechelen
PHOTOGRAPHY / Koen Vanmechelen
Curator / Peter Noever, Luo Yiping
LOCATION / Guangzhou, China

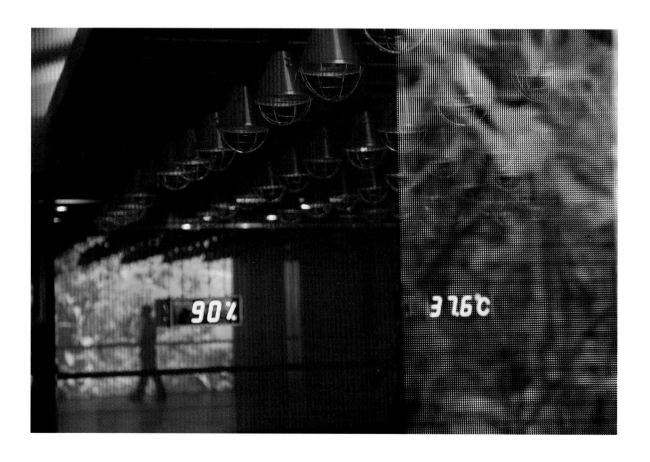

CERN required a new attraction: the exhibition Universe of Particles designed by ATELIER BRÜCKNER. It becomes a starting point for the many thousands of visitors who arrive each year, curious about the unique underground particle physics experiments taking place under the French-Swiss border near Genèva.

While the LHC is operating there is no public access to the experiments, so the exhibition answers many of the visitor's questions while also evoking a sense of wonder and awe at the remarkable scientific and engineering accomplishments and the mysterious worlds being revealed by the scientific work taking place at CERN.

Research at CERN is concerned with both the infinitely small and the incredibly large. The visitors experience a world without scale, at once encompassing the sub-atomic level and the vastness of the solar system. Entering the exhibition space, they enter another world. Here nothing is recognizable from the world outside.

All of the spherical designed elements in the space appear seamless, perfect. Nothing is familiar or expected. The visitor sees no plasma screens or touch-terminals, no display cases or graphic panels. Instead they experience projections seemingly in space, 3D digital objects within spheres, and beautifully lit concealed artifacts slowly revealed. Besides the spherical design, the uniformly neutral white color of the Corian surfaces and a swirling light circle at the base of every display is the connecting design language. The designers created light shades which lift the displays out and let them float apparently freely in the room.

CERN I Universe of Particles
ATELIER BRÜCKNER

DESIGN / ATELIER BRÜCKNER
PHOTOGRAPHY / Michael Jungblut
LOCATION / Genève, Switzerland

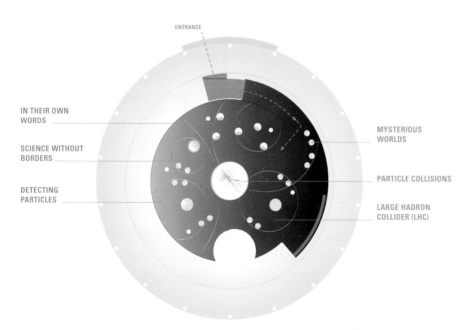

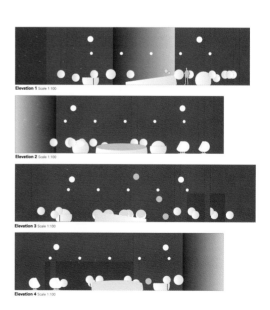

Ice Cube is a multimedia exhibition section presenting the contribution of the International Polar Foundation in Belgium to the international climate research world at the 2010 Shanghai Expo. The showcase is conceived as an abstract piece of ice. Through big openings in the facade the visitor has insight into two projects: Princess Elisabeth Antarctica (PEA), an emission-free polar base station, and Polaris Climate Change Observatory (PCCO), a planned science center for communicating polar research in Brussels. In the crevasse a sheet of real ice brings the visitor a sensory experience from the world of the poles.

Ice Cube
ATELIER BRÜCKNER

DESIGN / ATELIER BRÜCKNER
PHOTOGRAPHY / Antje Quiram, Stuttgart
LOCATION / Shanghai, China

The design of the House of Bols entailed a strategy involving concept, design and content being realized in films, interactive applications, graphics and a custom-made soundtrack. The result can be described as sensual and provocative - a spectacular combination of tastes, scents and colors, aimed at engaging the visitors' senses through exposure to a selection of aromas, music, videos, herbs and spices. The world of cocktails activates your senses while you discover all there is to know about one of the oldest companies in the Netherlands.

The House of Bols cannot be categorized as a museum or brand attraction, but is in fact a fascinating 600m² experience in its own right. The architecture of the building presented a range of challenges to the designers, as structural walls could not be moved. The team of designers has succeeded in making the most of a seemingly limited space by turning the space into an exciting and functional designed environment.

House of Bols, across Van Gogh Museum
…,staat creative agency

DESIGN / …,staat creative agency
PHOTOGRAPHY / …,staat creative agency
LOCATION / Amsterdam, the Netherlands

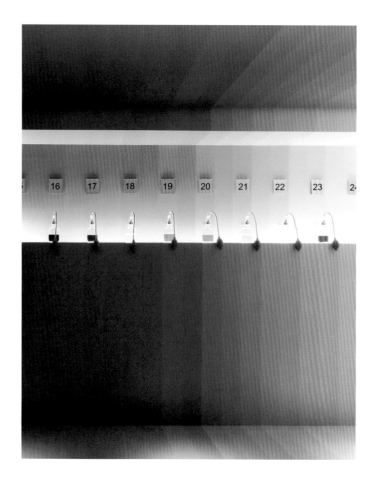

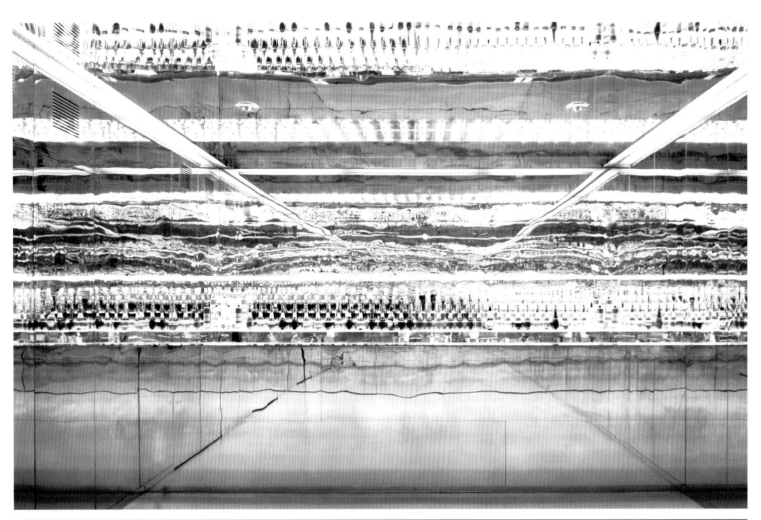

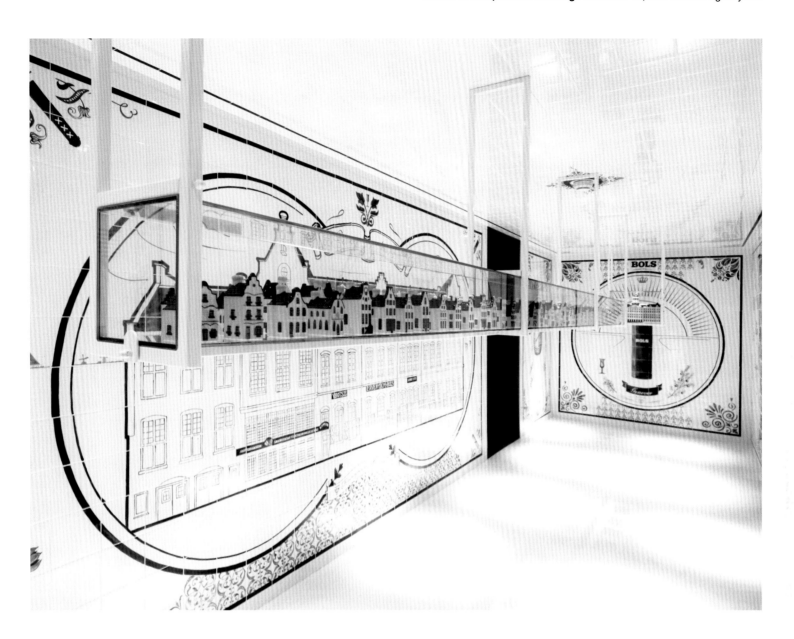

As part of the 50th year anniversary of the "Milano Salone", TORAFU was invited to design the Canon exhibition.

The installation, designed to the theme of "NEOREAL WONDER", was to include the application of the company's digital imaging technology. The designers were influenced by how light, normally formless, can appear as "light forms" before the spectators' very eyes when dust is illuminated in the dark. The designers wanted to build a new relationship with light, so by tracing the radiating light beams with countless strings, the light is artificially given substance. Density of the strings creates image screens that stretch across the space. These string screens differ from traditional flat screens as they can take on a variety of expressions. A new reality could be experienced through the mysterious unity of light and images, blending inside a space that is neither virtual nor real. The word "WONDER" was set up on the entrance wall as though it had been woven together by the countless strings on the reverse side. These are the strings that appeared to capture the constantly moving light, weaving it inside the space.

Light Loom
TORAFU ARCHITECTS

DESIGN / TORAFU ARCHITECTS
PHOTOGRAPHY / Daici Ano, Daisuke Ohki, Daisuke Shimokawa
LOCATION / Milan, Italy

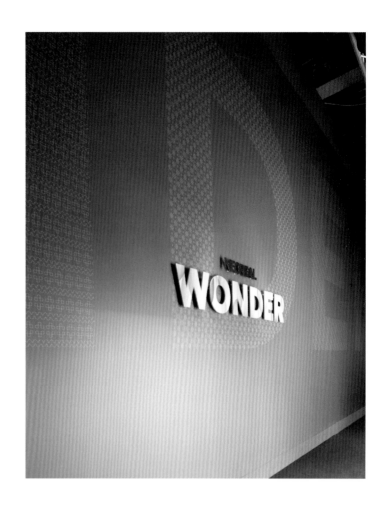

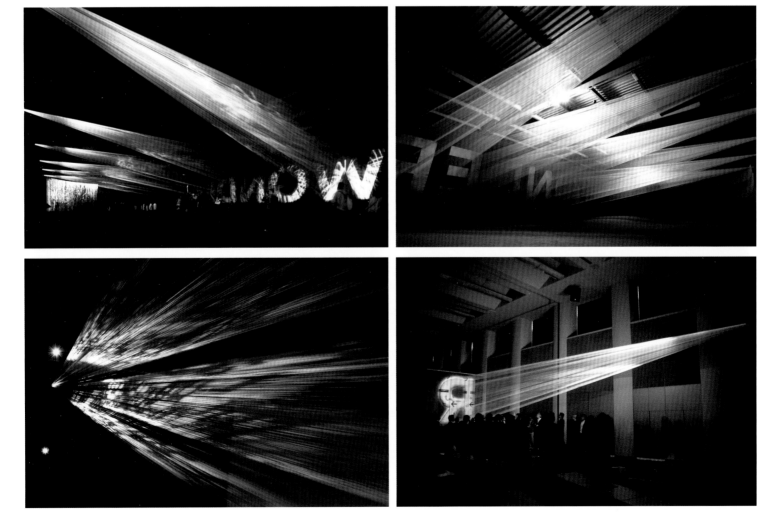

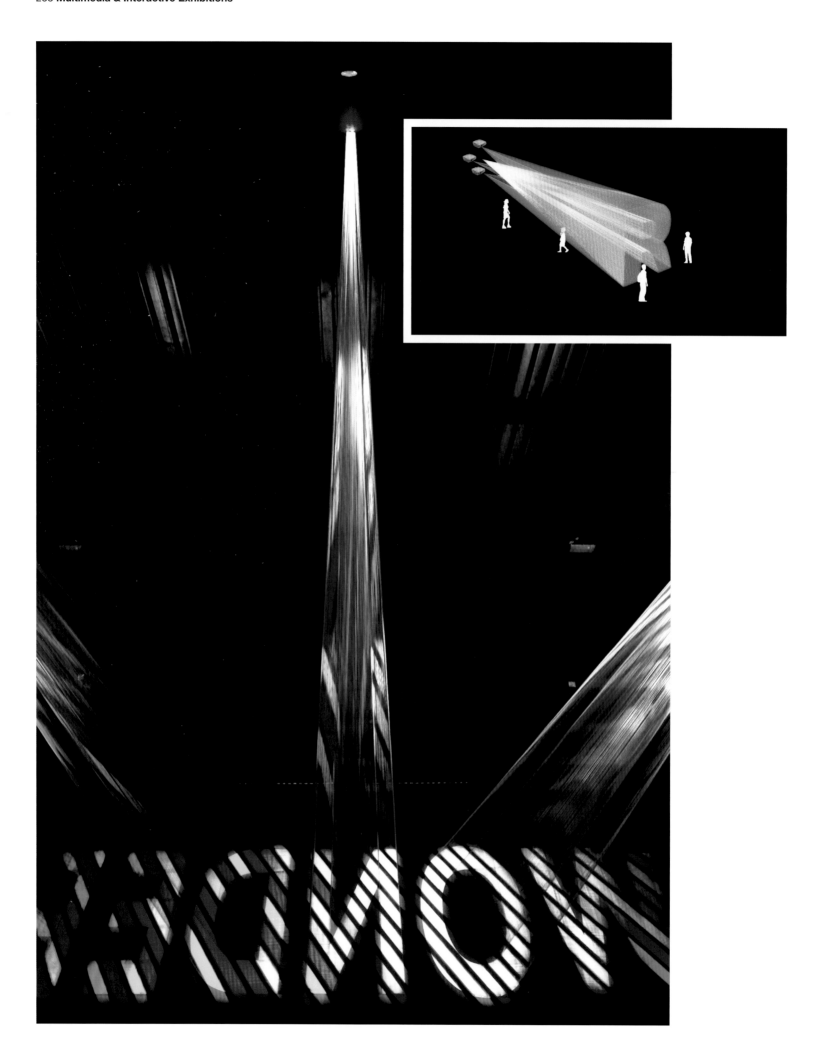

This airvase installation was created in the atrium at the back of the Spiral Building event space in Aoyama, Tokyo for the Paper Products Exhibition held from September 11 to 23, 2010. With a cloud of suspended white airvases fluttering overhead and an array of vases with diverse dotted patterns and colors arranged on a table below, the installation's 600 airvases captured the atmosphere of the venue in an attempt to express the image of Spiral's 25th anniversary. Visitors could enjoy the various designs as if taking a playful round-trip excursion by looking at the objects on a large round table positioned to fit in with the spiral slope that surrounds this event space. People crowded the lively workshops held during the staging of the exhibition, using pure white airvases as canvases for creating their own designs.

SPIRAL MARKET LIMITED SELECTION

TORAFU ARCHITECTS

DESIGN / TORAFU ARCHITECTS
PHOTOGRAPHY / Fuminari Yoshitsugu, Motoyuki Kihara, Hideki Ookura
LOCATION / Tokyo, Japan

INDEX

...,staat creative agency
Amsterdam, the Netherlands
www.staatamsterdam.nl

...,staat is a creative agency based in Amsterdam, which opened its doors in the magic millennium year 2000. With a background in the music scene, ...,staat's secret is a mix of 25 people. And a solid base of preferred parties. Everybody always works in different teams. ...,staat exists of strategists, art directors, copywriters, visual artists, digital thinkers, architects, PR and producers.

Besides global accounts, ...,staat also works on small and unusual projects.

...,staat loves the mix, and creativity is their platform.

p252-255

Anastasia Karandinou
UK
www.athensbysound.gr
www.karandinou.com

Anastasia Karandinou, Dr.,Architect Engineer NTUA, MSc Advanced Arch. Design, PhD on Sonic, Ephemeral and Hybrid design, Univ. of Edinburgh.

- Lecturer in Arch. Design, Univ. of Portsmouth and practicing architect.
- Invited juror and speaker in international arch. workshops.
- UIA 'Light of tomorrow' International competition award.
- Publications in academic journals and design magazines, international prizes and distinctions.

p212-215

Apostrophys the Synthesis Server Co., Ltd.
Bangkok, Thailand
www.apostrophys.com

Apostrophys is "multi-disciplinary design studio" that works in the segment of 'New media Technology' offering

more information channels to consumers, with the close integration of visual design, motion graphics, animation, game applications, lighting programming design, media technology, installation art features, interiors and architecture.

Their work features on events and exhibitions, parties, concerts, interior design, architecture design, visual design, feature and interactive technology.

p78-79, p80-83, p84-87, p96-99

ATELIER BRÜCKNER
Stuttgart, Germany
www.atelier-brueckner.com

Guided by its philosophy "form follows content", ATELIER BRÜCKNER sees its mission as the consistent production of spatial concepts from the content they are engaged to explore. ATELIER BRÜCKNER provides concept, planning, and implementation of content-generated architecture. The focus of the firm is on scenographically inspired projects for museums, exhibitions and expos.

ATELIER BRÜCKNER was established in 1997 by architect and stage designer Uwe R. Brückner and architect Shirin Frangoul-Brückner. Today it is run by them together with architect Prof. Eberhard Schlag and architect Britta Nagel. With more than 70 employees from nine different professions, it is now one of the world's leading ateliers for exhibition design and scenography.

p50-53, p244-247, p248-251

Basalt Architects
Iceland
www.basalt.is

Basalt architects hold quality practices, good service and artistic creativity paramount. Their works strive to take the environment into account and are well suited to local conditions and nature.

p194-195

BIG I Bjarke Ingels Group
Copenhagen, Denmark
www.big.dk

BIG is a young architectural company, characterized by an entrepreneurial spirit, true team-work across expertise areas and new ways of approaching conventional tasks. They have an informal work environment where camaraderie and collegial support are highly valued and where ambition, very high work morale and dedication to being the innovators of their field unify the staff. The firm is characterized by creativity, high energy and a unifying team spirit. The headquarters are located in Copenhagen and 18 months ago they started an affiliate in New York.

p62-63

BIG-GAME
Lausanne, Switzerland
www.big-game.ch

BIG-GAME was created in 2004 by Elric Petit (Belgian), Grégoire Jeanmonod (Swiss) and Augustin Scott de Martinville (French). They are graduates of ECAL (Lausanne) and La Cambre (Brussels), where they all studied industrial design. BIG-GAME is now based in Lausanne.

"The trio is known for its distinctive take on playful functionalism". They create objects for Moustache (F), Karimoku (JP) and Galerie Kreo (F). BIG-GAME was awarded the first prize of the "Die Besten" competition in 2005 and the Swiss federal design award in 2006 and 2010.

p106-107

Black Design
Singapore
blackdesign.com.sg

Black's approach focuses on the creation of value through design. Their sole purpose is to create design ideas that generate social, cultural, commercial, artistic, intellectual and emotional value.

Black's collaborative process with leading international artists, architects, designers, illustrators, business leaders and institutions allows them to constantly develop diverse projects that span across branding, graphic design, environmental design, exhibition curation and design, cultural content development, publishing, motion graphics and product design.

p158-159, p180-183

büromünzing 3d kommunikation
Stuttgart, Germany

www.bueromuenzing.de

büromünzing designer+architekten was founded by Uwe Münzing in Stuttgart in 1999. The office specializes in the design of museums and exhibitions featuring technical, cultural and historical content, as well as the presentation of brands and the development of space concepts that meet a wide variety of requirements. Having garnered many awards, their works follow a holistic approach to solutions that integrate architecture, design, media and visual communication. The company transforms and brings to life complex relationships in a balanced blend of aesthetic perception and communication of content.

p130-133

Cadaval & Sola-Morales
Spain/Mexico

www.ca-so.com

Cadaval & Sola-Morales was founded in New York City in 2003 and moved to both Barcelona & Mexico City in 2005. The studio operates like a laboratory in which research and development are seen as an important element of the design process. The mandate of the firm is to

create intelligent design solutions at many different scales, from large scale projects to small buildings, from objects to city fractions. Cadaval & Sola-Morales have completed built projects in the United States, Spain and Mexico.

p142-145

Cheungvogl Architects Ltd.
Hong Kong, China

www.cheungvogl.com

Cheungvogl is a multilingual and multicultural international design studio founded by Judy Cheung and Christoph Vogl after their contributions to Lord Norman Foster's headquarters in London, UK. Cheungvogl has participated in more than 100 projects varying in scale across Europe, North America, Asia and the Middle East, which include Wembley Stadium in London, Anfa Plage in Morocco, Sama Dubai Towers in Melbourne, Queen Alia International Airport in Jordan, Madison Avenue Tower in New York, Centralized Science Laboratories in Hong Kong and University of Pennsylvania Student Housing.

p28-29

Christina Achtypi
UK

www.athensbysound.gr
www.divercityarchitects.com

Christina Achtypi: Architect Engineer, N.T.U.A, MArch in Advanced Architectural Design, Bartlett, UCL, MSc in Computing & Design, UEL. RIBA chartered member. Partner in Divercity London.

Distinctions: Two 1st international prizes, one commendation.

p212-215

Culdesac
Spain

www.culdesac.es

CuldesacTM develops creative ideas for the sole purpose of adding value and business to brands.

Their clearly innovative character and a unique methodology based on a combination of strategy, creativity and first-class design allows us to create homologated projects.

p44-45

dan pearlman
Markenarchitektur GmbH
Berlin, Germany

www.danpearlman.com

dan pearlman is a strategic creative agency for brand strategy, brand communication and brand presentation in terms of holistic brand management.

Their goal is to anchor brands and experiences in the hearts and souls of the people. To deliver this they combine an extensive, strategic competence with high-level creativity in implementation. In action they take a 360° approach. They cover the entire spectrum, from strategic positioning and developing creative ideas for brands to implementing them in design and media, retail and brand experiences as well as architecture for zoos, hospitality and leisure environments.

p40-43, p64-67, p70-71

Emerystudio
Melbourne, Australia

www.emerystudio.com

The cross-disciplinary team at Emerystudio is led by Garry Emery and Bilyana Smith and numbers around 25 people.

Emerystudio are a Melbourne based design practice working across Australia, Asia Pacific, Middle East, United Kingdom and Northern Africa. The work of the practice has been extensively exhibited, published and awarded almost everywhere.

EXITDESIGN
Barcelona, Spain
www.exitdesign.com

EXITDESIGN is a Barcelona design & consulting company. A space for shared values. A common understanding of design. Design as a language, a method, a capacity. A capacity to change things: brands, products, technologies, spaces. A capacity to create new experiences.

FARM
Singapore
www.farm.sg

FARM is a cross disciplinary design practice. They are a curatorial team and a community-centered arts organization. They call themselves FARM because they would like to cultivate a culture of imagination. Underpinning all they do is a belief that joyful creativity is essential in all lives. FARM endeavors to share with you that delight in each of our projects.

Since 2005, FARM has worked on community projects which promote the arts. They organize national public art competitions and events. They arrange free quarterly talks by designers and artists.

Focus Lighting
New York, USA
focuslighting.com

Focus Lighting is an award winning professional architectural lighting design firm located in New York City. Since 1987, Focus Lighting have

continually created unique and successful lighting design solutions for projects of all sizes including hotels, resorts, retail, restaurants, museums, nightclubs, offices, and private residences around the world.

Franken Architekten GmbH
Germany
www.franken-architekten.de

Between the virtual and the real: Franken Architekten combines architectural practice with the opportunities for communication within a space, be it in the design for a temporary trade fair presentation or classic building construction.

The environments created by Franken Architekten use insights into the virtual world and go far beyond functionality: They create narrative spaces. Development of concepts and realization of corporate architecture, office buildings, retail, hotels and gastronomy, urban planning, residential buildings, museums, exhibitions, trade fair presentations, corporate design, installations, theme and brand worlds.

Hector Ruiz Velazquez
Madrid, Spain
www.ruizvelazquez.com

Hector Ruiz-Velazquez has a degree in architecture from the University of Virginia, USA, with studio professors from Harvard University and Columbia University. He founded his own architectural office in 1992 as a culmination of an extensive professional practice that includes architectural projects of a large scale, as well as corporate identities. A characteristic of his studio is its diversity not only culturally but also regarding the professional disciplines. The studio covers projects from urbanism to graphic

design, industrial and interior design, photography, as well as integral corporate images.

Heller Designstudio
Stuttgart, Germany
www.heller.tv

Heller Designstudio is a multidisciplinary designstudio focusing on architecture, design and media, based in Stuttgart, Germany. Their goal is to develop integrated design solutions with continuous aesthetics-ranging from graphic design to medial staging. The architects, communication designer and programmer together create immersive spaces in trade fairs, public spaces and architecture. Internet, video, 3D-animation and graphic design are used dynamically.

Ingrid Heijne Interior Design
Amsterdam, the Netherlands
www.ingridheijne-interiordesign.com

Ingrid Heijne Interior Design provides interior design services to both businesses and individuals. They take care of the total concept for each room, from idea to realization. They carefully attune the concept to the clients' wishes and requirements using their unique style and distinctive imagery, and then create a design that suits the clients' identity and personality to a tee. To reinforce the personality of the clients' interior, they design unique wall visuals, (wall) objects and folding screens that fit in perfectly with the style and ambience of the whole concept. By arranging elements, like furniture, paintings, objects and lighting, they create an atmosphere in which harmony and subtle amazement set the overtone.

Ippolito Fleitz Group – Identity Architects
Stuttgart, Germany
www.ifgroup.org

Peter Ippolito

MANAGING PARTNER. Study of architecture in Stuttgart and Chicago. Worked with Studio Daniel Libeskind, Berlin. Assistant to Prof. Ben Nicholson, Chicago. 1999 formation of zipherspaceworks. 2001-2002 Guest professor at the Art Academy Stuttgart. Since 2002 ippolito fleitz group. 2004-2008 teaching position at the University of Stuttgart. 2009 teaching position at the University of Biberach.

Gunter Fleitz

MANAGING PARTNER. Study of architecture in Stuttgart, Zürich and Bordeaux. Worked with Steidle+Partner, München. Project management for the Federal Supreme Court Leipzig for Prof. Stübler. 1999 formation of zipherspaceworks, since 2002 ippolito fleitz group.

p36-39, p46-49, p72-77

J. MAYER H Architects
Berlin, Germany
www.jmayerh.de

Founded in 1996 in Berlin, Germany, J.MAYER H Architects' studio focuses on works at the intersection of architecture, communication and new technology. Recent projects include a student center at Karlsruhe University, the villa Dupli.Casa near Ludwigsburg, Germany and the redevelopment of the Plaza de la Encarnacion in Sevilla, Spain, the office building ADA1 in Hamburg, Germany and the extension of the science park in Danfoss, Denmark. From urban planning schemes and buildings to installation work and objects with new materials, the relationship between the human body, technology and nature forms the background for a new production of space.

p224-227

Jangled Nerves
Stuttgart, Germany
www.janglednerves.com

Jangled Nerves designs and produces communication solutions at the crossing point between media and space, which are understood as two mutually interacting components. With this approach Jangled Nerves combines the functions of a creative agency and a media production firm.

The goal is to interweave architecture, graphic design, film, interaction and kinematics: all classical forms of media production are embedded into the spatial context, while stories are told in direct alignment with the targeted group. Hence, immersive and holistic experimental environments are created.

p196-197

Karim Rashid
New York, USA
www.karimrashid.com

Karim Rashid is one of the most prolific designers of his generation. Over 3000 designs in production, over 300 awards and working in over 35 countries attest to Karim's legend of design. His award winning designs include democratic objects and interiors. Karim's work is featured in 20 permanent collections and he exhibits art in galleries worldwide. Karim is a perennial winner of the Red Dot award, Chicago Athenaeum Good Design award, I.D. Magazine Annual Design Review, and IDSA industrial Design Excellence Award.

p24-27

Kasia Jezowska
London, UK
www.kasiajezowska.com

Kasia is a Polish-born, London-based curator and researcher specializing in

contemporary design and design exhibition history. Currently she is pursuing her PhD degree in History of Design at the Royal College of Art. Design Faction has been developed in partnership with the British Council and primarily shown at the Lodz Design Festival, Poland.

p232-235

KEGGENHOFF I PARTNER
Germany
www.keggenhoff.de

The rooms and buildings which KEGGENHOFF design on behalf of developers in Germany and around the world can be described very clearly – purposeful, emotional and functional. The main work of the office is the development and production of complete concepts in the fields of interior design, architecture and corporate architecture. Projects of varying sizes are completed with exemplary flexibility, striking a fine balance between concept, design and technical production. A wide range of renowned awards reflects the extremely high quality of the company's work.

p14-15, p16-19, p20-23

Koen Vanmechelen
Belgium
www.koenvanmechelen.be

The Belgian artist Koen Vanmechelen (1965) is an internationally renowned conceptual artist. His groundbreaking work deals with diversity and identity. Over the past decade Vanmechelen has collaborated with scientists from different disciplines. That earned him an honorary doctorate at the University of Hasselt this year.

p240-243

Kollision
Denmark
www.kollision.dk

Kollision Architecture Office was founded in July 2000. Works of Kollision include projects in architecture and urban development, and research and development of new methods and tools to involve citizens and users. Many of their projects integrate and develop information and communication technologies in the spatial and architectural contexts - from the design process to the design itself. A third core competency is the design and development of exhibition concepts, interactive installations and technological prototypes.

p62-63

Lise Lefebvre
Amsterdam, the Netherlands
www.liselefebvre.com

Lise Lefebvre is part textile artist and part product designer, with a big scoop of fun and a pinch of irreverence. Lise Lefebvre draws, paints, cuts, stitches, melts, knits, bakes, sprays, weaves, molds, and generally makes things for enjoyment and sometimes for others' enjoyment. From 3D knitwear prototyping to casting porcelain and designing with food, ropes, or other ancient carpets, she spends her days happily experimenting in her sunny Amsterdam studio. She also teaches design at Willem de Kooning Academy in Rotterdam.

p186-189

Maxime Mørel
Buenos Aires, Argentina
maximemorel.com

Maxime Mørel graduated from the Design Academy of Eindhoven. He is a highly creative and motivated designer, with a

sharp eye for detail, currently based in Buenos Aires, Argentina. He has been making design installations raising questions concerning representation and archiving and has exhibited his work worldwild in design galleries, fairs, and museums.

p186-189

MO KA
Brussels, Belgium
www.moka.be

Mo ka is a Brussels based design agency. Mo ka creates emotional experiences for premium brands. Since 2003 Mo ka has been creating concepts with a strong visual impact, combining a relentless creative drive with solid commercial experience. On their client list you'll find brands like Sony, Coca-Cola and Magnum.

p30-31

morePlatz
Rotterdam, the Netherlands
www.moreplatz.com

morePlatz is a collaboration of Caro Baumann and Johannes Schele that has existed for more than ten years. Their approach focuses on the usage of the city and its living conditions. Each project aims for innovation and development of spatial or programmatic qualities of the city. 'morePlatz' stands for 'more – refined – space'.

p138-141

MVRDV
Rotterdam, the Netherlands
www.mvrdv.nl

MVRDV was set up in Rotterdam, the Netherlands in 1993 by Winy Maas, Jacob van Rijs and Nathalie de Vries. MVRDV engages globally in providing solutions to contemporary architectural and urban

issues. Realized projects include the Dutch Pavilion for the World EXPO 2000 in Hannover. Recently MVRDV won the competition for the 30,000m^2 China Comic and Animation Museum in Hangzhou. A branch office in Shanghai opened earlier this year.

Together with Delft University of Technology MVRDV runs The Why Factory, an independent think tank and research institute providing an argument for architecture and urbanism by envisioning the city of the future.

p154-157

NAU
Switzerland/Germany
www.nau.coop

NAU is a multidisciplinary collective of designers. They are architects, art directors, interactive designers, visual effects artists and filmmakers. Their experience spans the spectrum from residential, hospitality and cultural design to advertising, games and Hollywood films. This unique mix allows them to create a team with talent tailored to realize the client's story.

p216-219

Nendo
Japan
www.nendo.jp

The concept of Nendo is to give people a small "!" moment. There are so many small "!" moments hidden in our everyday lives. But we don't always recognize them, and even when we do recognize them, we tend to unconsciously reset our minds and forget what we've seen. But we believe these small "!" moments are what make our days so interesting, so rich. That's why Nendo want to reconstitute the everyday by collecting and reshaping experiences into something that's easy to understand. Nendo like the people who've encountered their designs to feel these small "!" moments intuitively. That's nendo's job.

Open Source Architecture
Montreal/Los Angeles/Tel Aviv
www.o-s-a.com

Open Source Architecture (O-S-A) is an international architectural firm dedicated to the development of pioneering design research. Located in Montreal, Los Angeles, and Tel Aviv, O-S-A's international nature is reflected in its business profile, integrating technologies and industries from partners around the world for the sake of architectural innovation. O-S-A undertakes architectural tasks that range from industrial design and interior design to residential and commercial buildings; all are devised and executed with the utmost care.

Overtreders W
Amsterdam, the Netherlands
www.overtreders-w.nl

Overtreders W is a spatial design agency, founded in 2006 by Reinder Bakker and Hester van Dijk, both graduates of The Design Academy in Eindhoven. Overtreders W design indoor and outdoor spaces such as interiors, exhibitions and small pavilions. Contemporary themes such as the changing landscape, social cohesion in neighborhoods and sustainability come up in their work. The complex assignments they encounter are translated into a clear and strong image.

Paul Cocksedge Studio
London, UK
www.paulcocksedge.co.uk

London based Paul Cocksedge Studio is the internationally acclaimed design practice of directors Paul Cocksedge and Joana Pinho. Notable for the design of concepts, installations, public art and exclusive interior objects, the Studio explores the limits of technology in order to create unique design experiences. With an interdisciplinary approach and an acute sense of quality, Paul Cocksedge Studio reinvents contemporary design as an event.

The Studio accepts commissions and consultancy work for a wide range of high-end clients, including luxury fashion labels, exclusive interiors manufacturers and major cultural institutions. Paul Cocksedge Studio is dedicated to building a sophisticated portfolio of unique pieces and projects of international repute.

Ricardo Bak Gordon
Portugal
www.bakgordon.com

Ricardo Bak Gordon is currently a visiting professor in the Master in Architecture at the Instituto Superior Técnico, Lisbon, and Visiting Teacher at the Universidad Camilo José Cela, Madrid. His work as an architect was presented in different exhibitions in Portugal, Spain, Italy, UK, Germany, Czech Republic, Mexico, Ecuador, Brazil and Macau China and published in prestigious special editions. He won the FAD Award for Architecture 2011 and was Portugal's representative at the Venice Biennale 2010 with Alvaro Siza, Carrilho da Graça and Aires Mateus. In the year 2000 he created the atelier Bak Gordon Arquitectos, where he currently works.

Schmidhuber + Partner
Munich, Germany
www.schmidhuber.de

The team of Schmidhuber + Partner architects, interior designers and designers possess the creative potential that lends the brand message a three-dimensional form. They see their work as a contribution to the overall image of a company - at trade fairs, in the business world and in the public eye. In short, they see it as tangible brand architecture. Their design concepts start at the interface of marketing, architecture and communication. They are an expression of Schmidhuber + Partner's strong design expertise and interdisciplinary approach. The result: unmistakable brand architecture and lasting corporate design on both a national and international level, recognized by multiple industry awards.

Slowscape Collective
London, UK
www.slowscape.co.uk

Slowscape was developed and built as a collaborative project between four London based designers. Stuart Franks, Christopher Kennedy and Ceri Williams met whist studying architecture at the Royal College of Art and in 2010 joined forces with Thomas Woods - a product design graduate from Central St Martins.

The team members share a passion for designing and constructing structures that delight through their unique form, adaptable functions and innovative palette of materials. Complementing traditional hands-on craftsmanship with computer aided production, the collective takes on design commissions at a range of scales to deliver considered and engaging projects.

SO Architecture
Israel
www.soarch.co.il

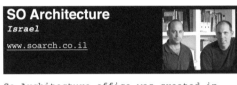

So Architecture office was created in 2007 by architect Shachar Lulav and architect Oded Rozenkier. These days the office works on several restaurants, public buildings, private houses, and architectural competitions. In all its work the office combines the work of graphic designers, landscape architects and industrial designers, and thus tries to reach excellence and creativity. The design of a project starts with metaphorical research and site analysis. Then Hand croquis, 3D software and physical models are constantly used in the design to reach the right architecture for the right place. So Architecture office is highly concerned with the worldwide ecological situation, so it is developing sustainable ideas that are executed in simple and costless ways.

p198-201

SOFTlab
New York, USA
www.softlabnyc.com

SOFTlab is a design studio based in New York City. The studio was created by Michael Szivos shortly after receiving a graduate degree in architecture from the Graduate School of Architecture, Planning and Preservation at Columbia University. The studio has since been involved in the design and production of projects across almost every medium, from digitally fabricated large-scale sculpture, to interactive design, to large-scale digital video installations.

p8-13

Solid Objectives – Idenburg Liu
New York, USA
www.so-il.org

Solid Objectives - Idenburg Liu (SO - IL) is an idea-based design office. With a global reach, it brings together extensive experience from the fields of architecture, academia and the arts. Founders Florian Idenburg and Jing Liu envisioned their New York-based studio in 2008 as a creative catalyst involved in all scales and stages of the architectural process. With roots in Europe, China and Japan – and sharing the optimism for architectural feasibility typical in those countries – Idenburg and Liu vehemently strive to realize their ideas in the world.

p116-117

SPAN/ del Campo, Manninger
Vienna, Austria
www.span-arch.com

SPAN/ del Campo, Manninger, focuses on the implementation of advanced, computational design techniques as well as on computer controlled fabrication methods. The practice has won numerous competitions and honors such as the Prize for Experimental Tendencies in Architecture. Among SPAN's best known designs is the Austrian Pavilion for the Shanghai Expo 2010. Matias del Campo and Sandra Manninger also focus on teaching architectural design in such schools as the Dessau Institute of Architecture, and the University of Applied Arts in Vienna. Currently Matias del Campo is teaching architectural design at UPenn, the University of Pennsylvania.

p134-135, p136-137

Studio Fabio Novembre
Italy
www.novembre.it

Born in 1966, Fabio Novembre became an architect in 1992. He cuts out spaces in the vacuum by blowing air bubbles, and makes gifts of sharpened pins so as to insure he never put on airs. His lungs are imbued with the scent of places that he's breathed, and when he hyperventilates it's only so he can remain in apnea for a while. As though he was pollen, he let himself go with the wind, convinced that able to seduce everything that surrounds him. He wants to breathe till he chokes and to love till he dies.

p100-103, p160-163, p202-205

Studio Makkink & Bey
Rotterdam, the Netherlands
www.studiomakkinkbey.nl

Designer Jurgen Bey and architect Rianne Makkink have operated Studio Makkink & Bey together in Rotterdam since 2002. The studio's many projects are diverse, and include public space projects, product design, architecture, exhibition design and applied arts. Aspects such as analyzing the content, the relationship between purpose and shape, design as a bearer of a story, and the relationship between spectators and bearers, designer and commissioner, can originate from exhibition design and architecture, but are also used in projects of other disciplines. Urban planning, architecture, and landscape architecture are inextricably bound to product design. The light bulb has had an influence on architecture, the way a house is built influences its interior, and a skyscraper could have never existed without the invention of the elevator.

p104-105

Stylianos Giamarelos
Athens, Greece
www.athensbysound.gr

Architect Engineer, MArch Theory of
Arch. Design NTUA, Ba and MA Philosophy
and History of Science and Technology
UoA, Urban Research Associate NTUA,
PhD candidate UCL. His awarded essays,
comics and projects have been published
in academic journals and international
conference proceedings.

p212-215

Tilman Thürmer
Berlin, Germany
www.shmog.org

Born in 1972 in Berlin, Germany, Tilman
Thürmer studied architecture at the
Berlin University of Arts. Since 1994 he
realized numerous exhibitions and museum
projects with Buero Thürmer, rendered
expert's reports and participated in
research projects in the field of museum
design. His activity focuses on the
conception and coordination of museum
exhibitions at the convergence of content
and design, such as the award winning
HNF in Paderborn, the largest computer
museum of the world and the Forum of
Contemporary History in Leipzig. In
conjunction with his office activities
he has taken part in various science
projects in the fields of virtual reality
and experimental media and museum
architecture.

p166-171

TORAFU ARCHITECTS
Tokyo, Japan
torafu.com

Founded in 2004 by Koichi Suzuno and
Shinya Kamuro, TORAFU ARCHITECTS employs
a working approach based on architectural
thinking. Works by the duo include a
diverse range of disciplines, from
architectural design to interior design
for shops, exhibition space design,
product design, spatial installations
and film making. They have received many
prizes including the Design for Asia (DFA)
Grand Award for the "TEMPLATE IN CLASKA"
in 2005, and the Grand Prize of the Elita
Design Awards 2011 with "Light Loom
(Milano Salone 2011)". The airvase book
and TORAFU ARCHITECTS Ideas + Process
2004-2011 were published in 2011.

p124-125, p126-129, p146-147, p148-149,
p150-153, p208-211, p256-259, p260-263

Universal Design Studio
London
www.universaldesignstudio.com

Universal Design Studio is recognized
as one of the world's most innovative
creative design consultancies. They
have a distinct, multi-disciplinary
approach towards the design of branded
environments. The team of architects,
interior designers and product designers
is committed to creating unique,
arresting, comprehensive environments
with an effective commercial purpose.
Universal was founded in London in 2001
by Edward Barber and Jay Osgerby to
augment their award-winning product and
furniture design folio.

p236-237

WISE Architecture
Seoul, Korea
www.wisearchitecture.com

WISE Architecture is a multi-cultural
design firm established by Young Jang and
Sook Hee Chun in 2008. The firm is based
in Seoul, Korea and offers architectural
design, interior design, programming and
space analysis, and master planning.
Our research based collaborative
approach creates end products that are
innovative and functional but which are
aesthetically pleasing and attentive to
environmental concerns. The designers
believe architecture is the medium to
cross-over the boundaries in between
times, spaces, arts, and people. It is
with passion that the projects they
visualize become realities.

p182-185

Zaha Hadid
London, UK
www.zaha-hadid.com

Zaha Hadid, founder of Zaha Hadid
Architects, was awarded the Pritzker
Architecture Prize (considered to be
the Nobel Prize of architecture) in
2004 and is internationally known for
both her theoretical and academic work.
Each of her dynamic and innovative
projects builds on over thirty years of
revolutionary exploration and research
in the interrelated fields of urbanism,
architecture and design. Hadid's interest
lies in the rigorous interface between
architecture, landscapes and human-made
systems, leading to experimentation with
cutting-edge technologies. Such a process
often results in unexpected and dynamic
architectural forms.

p120-123

ACKNOWLEDGEMENTS

We would like to thank all of the designers involved for the kind permission to publish their works, as well as all of the photographers who have generously granted us the right to use their images. We are also very grateful to many other people whose names do not appear in the credits but who made specific contributions and provided support. Without these people, we would not have been able to share these beautiful works of fair, special event, and art exhibition design with readers around the world.